THE DOORS
OF DECEPTION

THE DOORS OF DECEPTION

DEFEAT THE ACTS OF DECEPTION

WRITTEN BY JAMILLE JUDGE

Copyright © 2025 by Jamille Judge

Scripture taken from the New King James Version. "Copyright © 1982 by Thomas Nelson". Used by permission All rights reserved.

All rights reserved. No part of this publication may be reproduced, distributed, or transmitted in any form or by any means, including photocopying, recording, or other electronic or mechanical methods, without the prior written permission of the copyright owner and the publisher, except in the case of brief quotations embodied in critical reviews and certain other noncommercial uses permitted by copyright law. For permission requests, write to the publisher, addressed "Attention: Permissions Coordinator," at the address below.

ARPress
45 Dan Road Suite 15
Canton, MA 02021

Hotline: 1(888) 821-0229
Fax: 1(508) 545-7580

Ordering Information:
Quantity sales. Special discounts are available on quantity purchases by corporations, associations, and others. For details, contact the publisher at the address above.

Printed in the United States of America.

ISBN-13:	Softcover	979-8-89676-334-5
	eBook	979-8-89676-335-2
	Hardback	979-8-89676-336-9

Library of Congress Control Number: 2025906540

DEDICATION

I thank the Lord God Almighty for keeping His promises and never leaving when others turned away.

I want to dedicate this book to my late Grandmother, MA, who has always supported me and the family. She was the glue that kept everything together. I cannot thank her enough for the countless words of wisdom she poured into me during the time of her life that matured me into the woman I have become today. The unlimited love she has shared for others has changed many lives. May her soul rest with the Most High.

I also want to thank my mother and aunt, who have supported me through different challenges, changes, and difficulties, no matter the rough places. Their insight and experiences have shaped me to weather the storms I have faced, and I will forever admire them.

Lastly but not least, I want to thank my readers, and Our Faith Heals Community for not only supporting me but also being a part of my journey. I will forever be grateful for the opportunity to pour my knowledge into this book. May this book be a blessing to you and anyone you have decided to share it with. I pray that God reveals truth and clarity to you. May God gift you with increased wisdom as you read through the pages. I appreciate the endless support.

TABLE OF CONTENTS

Dedication i
Introduction v
Chapter 1 – The Sprouts 2
Chapter 2 – How It Is 8
Chapter 3 – What A Liar 18
Chapter 4 – People Play 24
Prayer For Discernment... 31
Chapter 5 – Mind Control 34
Chapter 6 – The Advantage 39
Chapter 7 – The Fight Against Deceit 44
Chapter 8 – At Its Core 49
Chapter 9 – It Is Spreading 56
Chapter 10 – Truth Seeker 62
Prayers For Truth Seekers And Carriers 65
Chapter 11 – I Understand 67
Chapter 12 – Self-Deception 78
Chapter 13 – Security 88
Repentance Prayer 93
Chapter 14 – Stand On It 96
Chapter 15 – We Conclude 100
Deceptive Practices 104
Prayer For Wisdom 106

Reflections	108
Write Your Own Prayer	116
Write Your Own Prayer	118
Affirmations	120
7 Day Self Prayers Against Deception	122
7 Day Self Prayers Against Deception	123
Day 1	123
7 Day Self Prayers Against Deception	124
Day 2	124
7 Day Self Prayers Against Deception	125
Day 3	125
7 Day Self Prayers Against Deception	126
Day 4	126
7 Day Self Prayers Against Deception	127
Day 5	127
7 Day Self Prayers Against Deception	128
Day 6	128
7 Day Self Prayers Against Deception	129
Day 7	129
Back Text	130
About The Author	131

INTRODUCTION

To those who have ears, let them hear.

I thank the Lord Almighty Jesus Christ for the opportunity to share this book with you. During my prayer times, He told me that deception is rampant in the world, causing suffering to His people due to the lack of seeking truth and wisdom. This book will equip you against the schemes of the enemy by keeping on the Full Armor of God; the Breastplate of Righteousness, the Shield of Faith, the Helmet of Salvation, Shoes with the preparation of the gospel of peace, the Belt of Truth, the Sword of the Spirit which is the Word of God, and through Prayer, Fasting and Supplication. During your walk with Christ, you must seek truth and clarity. So, you are not judging a book by the cover, not living in a lie, deceiving yourself or others, or seeking validation Outside of God's Hand.

We live in an era in time where the Media has controlled the minds of the masses to think that what we see on these platforms is the entire truth without prayer, confirmation, research, clarity, or understanding. Word of mouth has become the only valued evidence of information in this society. Because of this, I have seen many reputations tarnished, lies spread, word curses formed, targeted sabotage, and self-destruction, all caused by this generation's lack of seeking truth. Let God be true and every man a liar if it comes up against the Knowledge of God.

If we do not diligently speak God's Word, we become defenseless against the world's powers. Fear has kept people in a stronghold, where most are afraid to use their voices if they go against the masses and their opinions, all while knowing what is true, just, and right. This state of mind causes mental bondage and oppression and is an open invitation to deception because they do not love the truth.

I have a question.

Where are the bold believers?

Bold enough to stand for what is Holy, right, pure, noble, and just in the sight of God no matter the popularity of a circumstance, liking, and its potential outcome. We made this book for you.

Before we begin, I recall the game "Chinese Whispers," where ten or more people sit in a circle, and one of the individuals starts the game by sharing something in the ear of the person next to them. The person receiving the message can share what was said initially or modify it with the next person. As they pass down the message to the individual next to them, the last person to receive it is to share what was said out loud. When it gets to the last person, it is not the original message initially shared. This game sheds light on how rumors start and how misinformation can spread. The catch to the game is that you don't know which person switched or modified the original message while in transition. Here is a prime example of how deception can form subtly in the reality of life.

Why is this?

1. People love to modify a message according to their liking, not the truth.

2. Some love to deceive others because of the attention it brings.
3. People love the image it carries.
4. Deception makes people feel better about themself, and it is more entertaining.
5. People enjoy mind control.
6. People love to take advantage of an opportunity.
7. People see the self-gain in a situation.
8. People cover their hatred with deceit.
9. The list goes on.

"He who hates, disguises *it* with his lips, And lays up deceit within himself;" Proverbs 26:24

This book will encourage you to use God-given discernment, wisdom, knowledge, power, and authority to withstand the troubles of opinion, lies, deceit, people's perceptions, projections, and any opposition set against you to fail. These demonic attempts against your destiny are to prevent you from ever acknowledging your God-given identity and purposely sent to stagnate you. You will discover the benefits of using the power of God to establish a firm foundation in your life so that you can remain anchored in the Word of God and His thoughts towards you so you do not fall victim to the agenda of deception. Deception can seem very smooth, like a snake wrapping itself around your foot, until you find yourself caught in a foothold and cannot escape.

Let us remember the enemy uses people to fulfill his desires on the earth.

"**Be sober, be vigilant; because your adversary the devil walks about like a roaring lion, seeking whom he may devour.**"
1 Peter 5:8

Before you get to the end of this book, you will learn the Do's & Don'ts:

1. Don't make conclusions without knowing the whole story.

2. Do use discernment and test every spirit.

3. Don't trust everyone's words and opinions.

4. Do apply wisdom in all situations.

5. Don't compare your life to someone's image.

6. Do ask the right questions.

7. Don't act on assumptions.

8. Do learn to empathize but not pity.

9. Don't rush your understanding.

10. Do validate everything with the Lord.

May this book be a blessing to you during your decision-making.

CHAPTER ONE

THE SPROUTS

CHAPTER 1 – THE SPROUTS

I wrote this book because experiencing the emotions after deception due to not knowing required years of healing. This experience affected how I felt, thought, and expressed myself, and I did not allow others into my inner circle. I was unaware that the deception would push me to become wiser and prepare me for what would come. I want to share what I have learned throughout the journey, while in my process of becoming in hopes that it may help guide your journey.

The sprout. Every seed someone waters will grow. If you sow seeds of love, you will reap a harvest of love. If you sow seeds of prosperity, you will reap a harvest of prosperity. If you sow seeds of jealousy, a person's character and actions will present a jealous person. If you sow seeds of hatred, the lifestyle and actions of a person will show hatred. You will know each person by their fruit. When people reveal themselves, believe them.

"[18] **A good tree cannot bear bad fruit, nor *can* a bad tree bear good fruit.** [19] **Every tree that does not bear good fruit is cut down and thrown into the fire.** [20] **Therefore by their fruits you will know them.**" Matthew 7:18-20

I recall a season when I strongly wanted people to be how I perceived them. This was a dangerous quality because when you wear your heart on your sleeve and only seek the good in people, you are setting yourself up for betrayal. I have learned that most people will show up in the most beneficial way for them, and when it is no longer helpful, they will resort to their natural habits or desires. Time will always reveal the character of others.

There are moments when it is hard to see people for who they truly are or where their interests lie. A person's actions must line up with what they say. When what you see is negated because you trust what is said to be moral, it is a red flag. The sprout will always show. The sprouts are ignored at times until they grow to become untamable. The sprout reveals true identity, involvements, participations, associations, intents, interests, and character. I am going to go through the sprouts.

For example, when you plant a tomato seed in a farm's yard, visitors are unaware of what will grow unless told. They would see nothing but the soil until the tomato grows. In the process, the seed will sprout and grow to reveal it is a tomato for visitors to see.

Like life, you may not immediately know people's motives and intentions, so you must always pray for discernment, observe, and accept what others show you. In all relationships, it matters what seeds they have sown in the past and the present because they will eventually sprout. There is always a potential personal effect without enlightenment. Many would be in better predicaments, situations, and circumstances had they known who someone indeed was or if they handled situations more delicately. Everyone's life can change in the blink of an eye because of people, as they can destroy your life if you let them. Although this is possible, it does not have to happen.

The sprout of association. The friend group is a key indicator of revealing personality. Those who have similarities will find a connection to one another. Being in the room with those you want to discern will be more evident as you hear their discussions and what intrigues them. Society people influence behaviors, mindsets, ways of living, and decision-making. Naturally, people desire to belong in spaces and communities and want to feel needed, but those who are not strong-minded can find themselves wrongly influenced by others because of this need. Most people would never admit to having a weak mind, but their decision-making will show you what you need to know. Associations matter. People will follow the decisions of their friend group or look for others to validate their choices. Connections can destroy or develop a person. Consider your friend groups and those friend groups connected to your friends.

Who are they connected with?

What decisions do they make?

How do they talk about others when they are in the room vs. when they are not?

What are their interests and priorities?

What validates them?

Are their associations developing or destructing?

The sprout of involvement and engagement is where you acknowledge where people spend their time and energy. Time spent speaks volumes about what they prioritize and where their focuses are maintained. Never connect with anyone with nothing to lose, as they will risk everything for a moment. A momentary gain for a lifetime of suffering is not worth it. Whenever anyone is explaining a situation, you must be aware of their associations, their role in the problem, and how they are maneuvering through the matter. Knowing this information can prevent deception because what one will do to another can be done to you. You can become self-deceived when you think you're an exception to someone's actions. I have seen people eat the words "It could never be me" mentality when connecting with those who mistreat others. **"Do not be deceived, God is not mocked; for whatever a man sows, that he will also reap." Galatians 6:7**

What do they participate in?

What roles do they play in situations?

Do they have anything to lose?

The sprout of interest. A person's interest can help determine their direction in life. Where their passions reside and what they enjoy will either be a warning or a blessing to know them. When people do not feel the confidence to accomplish their goals, they enjoy and laugh at destroying others' lives, relationships, successes, assets, and plans. They also find laughter in others' pain. A lack of self-worth, dedication to destruction, and pain that lingers into bitterness and resentment all play a part. Anyone who gains satisfaction at the destruction or defeat of another person you must be mindful of their presence. If their interests are self-absorbed and they overshadow the consideration of the effects they have on others, including instant gratification, you must be mindful. You can tell a lot about a person based on their enjoyment. Compromised people are prevalent and can switch on you at any moment.

What do they enjoy?

What are their passions?

The sprout of intent. People come with all types of intentions and motives, known and unknown. Deception forms from hidden intent and secret agendas. Everyone has something that drives them from and to. Not all drives stem from positivity and goodwill. Let's discuss some negative drives: selfishness, jealousy, retaliation, trauma, and anger cause ill intentions. Have you ever tried to figure out why someone would crush and take advantage of the heart of a good person? There is something that is driving the ill motive. Selfishness plays a significant part in ill intent because a selfish person does not factor in or consider the damage they create on others, only their mission. Their actions are a reflection of them, what they aim to project onto others, and how they want them to feel. Through prayer, God will reveal the intents of man and what no one else sees. Wicked people thrive in secrecy, but you are called to be a light. Your life is important to God, and deception should not be able to stand in your presence.

The sprout of character, morals, principles, and values are subject to all attacks if you do not stand by them. When I discern the character of others, I am looking at the environment they create in their atmosphere. The Bible says it rains on the just and the unjust (Matthew 5:45), so what environment do they create in tough times despite the circumstances? It helps me to discern their maturity level. I consider how people treat those they don't need. Movements matter. What do they do when no one is looking? Integrity is a quality many lack when compromised with what they say, do, and act. Good characteristics to observe are respect, honor, trustworthiness, consideration, honesty, pure heart, encouragement, and dedication while being Holy Spirit-filled with a God-fearing foundation. When you hold yourself to such a standard, you are careful around those who do not.

You must know those with negative characteristics, such as liars, manipulators, self-absorbers, wicked, confusers, thieves, cheaters, and deceivers. If a liar believes a lie would cause a "better" outcome, they will lie. Deceivers are not concerned with the person they are lying to or about; they are just worried about the outcome. I have learned not to take things personally because I am aware of the times.

I have named some of the different sprouts you must be mindful of so you are not left heartbroken once the true colors are revealed. People will show you what they want you to know or how much they think you do, which is why you must pray, discern, and observe the patterns of people.

People can change if they want to, and their decision is in the hands of the beholder. There is beauty in a changed mind, but many do not want to place the effort forth to change. We must accept those who made their decision and their bed.

CHAPTER TWO

HOW IT IS

CHAPTER 2 – HOW IT IS

Deception is spiritual. It is satan's tactic, a tool planted in the minds of the enemy's camp to cause havoc on the earth. The sprouts are what to notice in the flesh, but the battle is spiritual. The battle is not against flesh and blood.

"So the great dragon was cast out, that serpent of old, called the Devil and Satan, who deceives the whole world; he was cast to the earth, and his angels were cast out with him." Revelation 12:9

We live in a World filled with wickedness, deception, confusion, malice, ill intent, and persuasion. These attacks are influenced by demonic activity in the regions, controlling the minds, bodies, and souls of the masses of people. This activity reveals very robotic behavior, actions, words, and emotions in others. No one knows how they feel, what to believe, and how to act. I say robotic because the actions of many are not self-dependent but base opinions on what others do and are led by deception. If people are aware and seek after truth, then they are in a more significant position to make sound decisions and defeat the powers of deception. It is OK not to know everything, but it is never OK to be ignorant in areas that can directly detrimentally affect your life and future.

Deception can form by perception and how you view life, situations, and circumstances. If you view life outside of God's vision, that is an entrance gate to being deceived and can push you away from the will of God. Do not participate in things God is not pleased with and go against the Word of God.

Believers, what are you coming into agreement with?

In 2023, God provided revelation to me and advised that many in the church do not prosper because of what they are coming into agreement with and the covenants created unknowingly. For example, if you see someone in need, and with your resources, God told you to help them, and you do not. Not only are you operating in disobedience, but you have come into agreement with this person's downfall. You had the resources but chose to watch them suffer and ignore the voice of God, and this action can stunt your breakthrough and blessings because of your disobedience and agreements.

"^{27} Do not withhold good from those to whom it is due, When it is in the power of your hand to do *so*. ^{28} Do not say to your neighbor, "Go, and come back, And tomorrow I will give *it*," When you have it with you." Proverbs 3:27-28

To agree with someone's downfall can also look like gossip, slander, spreading false information, and ignorance. Everyone loves to use the famous "I did not know" speech after making a mistake and wanting to prevent the consequences. "I did not know" cannot get you out of the covenants you created, and you are still considered guilty of the action. You will need deliverance by repentance, denouncing, and renouncing.

"If a person sins, and commits any of these things which are forbidden to be done by the commandments of the LORD,

though he does not know *it,* **yet he is guilty and shall bear his iniquity." Leviticus 5:17**

Perception can influence your point of view. How you regard, understand, and interpret information can influence your attitude, actions, and emotions towards it. If your perspective of life and how you see people are tarnished, you can be deceived.

Deception can sneak into your life through an identity crisis, a lack of identity, and what you do not know. When you have no firm authority on what you do and do not stand for, what you will and will not do gives the enemy legal rights to attack your mind, which are never addressed. When mind battles are only tamed, they can erupt back stronger at any time again in your life.

A lack of control over one's mind can cause you to be easily persuaded, confused, and attached to almost anything. We live in a monkey-see, monkey-do world, including industries, platforms, environments, popularity, and influence.

Here's an issue in today's society figuratively: if a person sees two boats on the dock, and the first boat is packed with people but the second boat has five people, naturally, people will gravitate towards the ship with the most people as that ride looks to be more "fun" and "entertaining."

Why is this an issue?

This is an issue because many will hop on the boat, and most people will not know or realize where the ship is heading until it is too late. When they finally realize the boat's direction and the ship starts to sink, everyone panics to escape.

Had they been aware of the boat's direction before just considering having fun and hopping on, they could have prevented themselves from entering and causing panic in their own lives. Here is an example of perception. The view of the boat with most people was deemed more engaging and entertaining, not realizing that the "fun" turned into "fate" quickly.

¹³ "Enter by the narrow gate; for wide *is* the gate and broad *is* the way that leads to destruction, and there are many who go in by it. ¹⁴ Because narrow *is* the gate and difficult *is* the way which leads to life, and there are few who find it." Matthew 7:13-14

Deception can look like the wrong point of view, wrong perception, persuasion, image, half-truths, wordplay, and word choices. Words are powerful. I repeat, words are powerful and they are compelling. The effect of words can cause lifelong trauma and damage that you can spend your entire life fighting off the word curses. Word curses do not just form from gossip, lies, and negative words spoken against you.

Word curses also form from manipulation and deception. These forms of word curses can cause delusion and bondage.

Many speak lightly on delusion and are quick to call someone delusional freely and openly. But if I can be honest, I have recently discovered that delusional disorder is a diagnosed mental disorder where you cannot decipher reality from imagination. Word curses in manipulation and deception happen with wordplay and word choices, and they can cause a false imagination of yourself. Some words are like paper cuts, where you barely see the cut, but the aftermath pain is excruciating. Words are not only words if they are spoken aloud and acted on. Once those words are spoken aloud in the atmosphere, you can not take them back. Yes, you can apologize for the words said, but the words now have life. Think about word scars and how what others have said still bothers people for years. Our tongue has power and can influence good or evil surrounding us. You spoke life or death in your words. I will shed more light on word curses in another chapter.

People deceive to appease the flesh, whether it be an image or an advantage. The aftermath of being misled is harmful, hurtful, damaging, shameful, and traumatizing.

People are easily satisfied by what others say, especially those they care for, because they long for it to be accurate and end up going down every avenue to find truth in their statement, even when there is none, and they are unsettled about it. The plot gets more prominent with this type of disbelief. At this point, it becomes self-deception.

Why must you make the story add up when it does not?

Self-deception occurs when we make things add up when they don't, and it is a problem. The pain is self-inflicting because we decided not to get clarity, not to ask the questions, not to pray on it. We chose to believe what we wanted and not verify what was said.

It is like someone who does not like you. Your generosity and kindness will not change that, no matter what you do or say when making a decision.

To believe anything without clarity, research, and understanding is a choice to be open to deception.

Social influencers' reputations can be damaged by others' decisions to believe things about them that are not true. This imagery has affected deals, promotions, opportunities, and ventures in their lives. It can also affect the individual's mindset and income streams if they are not strong enough to resist the powers of deception.

I will tackle the demonic powers of deception, lies, manipulation, and insecurities in this book because if they are not dealt with and addressed, destruction comes at the hands of people and the spirits operating in them.

Time is the missing factor. You cannot be quick to jump to conclusions, have all the answers, and live for instant gratification and a fast life. People easily retain false information because they do not allow time to verify the provided information. They will run, repeat, and share it with the world, not the person it is about. Instead of clarifying the information provided, they share it like a bag of candy, which is unfortunate.

Do not be quick to believe a message without testing the fruit of the sender and their character.

The 9 Fruit of the Spirit are:

Love

Joy

Peace

Longsuffering

Kindness

Goodness

Faithfulness

Gentleness

Self-Control

"²² But the fruit of the Spirit is love, joy, peace, longsuffering, kindness, goodness, faithfulness, ²³ gentleness, self-control. Against such there is no law." Galatians 5:22-23

What fruits are they bearing?

Do you test their words?

Do their actions line up with what they say?

Are they producing fruit of the Spirit?

When you do not test the spirit of a person providing a message, you can operate in error if the information is not clear or accurate. Inaccurate information brings mistakes, guilt, problems, pain, patterns, and suffering. You must allow time for God to reveal the truth. Cry out to the Lord and pray for the Holy Spirit, who will guide you into all truth.

Just as we desire to believe our loved ones when they share a story with us, we should have the same desire with God to provide insight. There is always a cause for deception.

When anyone provides information to you and desires your feedback or intervention in a situation, you must be attentive to the actual cause. Identifying the cause can prevent unnecessary stress, trauma, pain, anxiety, problems, and so much more. The Lord gives you wisdom to protect, prevent, and guide. When you are not pulling on the Holy Spirit for guidance, you become vulnerable and immune to the enemy's attack against you. Everyone will be immune, like an attack on the body that is destroying from the inside.

Every demonic spirit needs a carnal body to influence expression. Once a person is possessed, they need deliverance to be free from the hold. Deception is a form of witchcraft and is considered demonic activity. Others may not view it as such, but it is much bigger than what meets the carnal eyes. They are not concerned with the effect it has on the people they influenced or the impact on the targeted purpose.

Using people for their resources is deception. Wrapping the truth with a lie is deception. Hiding or covering the truth is deception. Manipulating minds is deception. Reverse psychology is deception. Masking true identity is deception. Sugar coating or sweeping truth under the rug is deception. Not having the whole story is deception. Being quick to spread a rumor or gossip is deceptive. Any false information made or encouraged to believe is true is deception.

This is how it is.

CHAPTER THREE

WHAT A LIAR

CHAPTER 3 — WHAT A LIAR

Women lie. Men lie. But the truth stands. Jesus is the Way, Truth, and the Life. You must walk in the truth wholeheartedly regardless of liking. Deceivers create lies for many reasons. Knowing the origin of a lie will help you understand why people tell it without blinking. God hates liars.

"16 These six *things* the LORD hates, Yes, seven *are* an abomination to Him: 17 A proud look, A lying tongue, Hands that shed innocent blood, 18 A heart that devises wicked plans, Feet that are swift in running to evil, 19 A false witness *who* speaks lies, And one who sows discord among brethren." Proverbs 6:16-19

People who do not like the truth love a lie because it makes them feel better. Lies are false statements, and people in society accept them without question. When communicating with a liar, you will find them switching up stories. The best way to expose this type of liar is by addressing the initial conversation and pointing out everything said differently. Call them out at the moment; you know they are lying. Although a lie is a lie, people lie differently and for different reasons. Some lie about everything, some lie about status, some lie out of habit, some lie for an escape, and some lie in certain circumstances for better outcomes.

If they lie, there is always a reason. The best way to catch a liar is to repeat what was said, address it truthfully, and watch their defensiveness. A liar never likes to be confronted about their lies or to know that someone does not believe them. It alerts and triggers a nerve that can cause them to act erratically, point the finger at someone else, or completely shut down.

I recall an associate who lied about everything from the places they traveled to, the money they had, and the "pretend" boyfriends. I mean, their stories sounded so realistic until the timeline of her stories did not add up. I realized people would lie to make their lives look better in the sight of other people. It makes them feel better about themselves to know someone believes what they have "accomplished." Indeed, a discerning person can see their insecurities, and they are seeking attention.

You can post a picture on social media claiming a luxury lifestyle, and to viewers, it looks like you are living your best life, but not at all. Although a picture is worth 1000 words, it doesn't explain your life story. For example, a couple could look happily in love on their media accounts, but this does not provide insight into what goes on in their home. People are quick to say, "couple goals."

In the same way, a liar can be good at lying, and you don't know their thoughts as they explain their "story." If you do not have discernment, you can be deceived, especially without knowing the purpose behind them sharing the story with you.

Deceivers use lying to try and cover up the truth, hide mistakes and intent, redirect attention and image, and persuade. These acts on the right person who believes them can cause deception, manipulation, and a reaction. Most of humanity runs with storylines, half stories, and advocates for false narratives.

Is anyone seeking truth these days or just seeking popularity?

Running with narratives is the invitation to include others in the shenanigans, whether beneficial or detrimental. Those who want involvement may have experience with rejection and a need for acceptance and validation.

Conversely, liars do not care how the lies they spread affect the lives of the people they tell and those who advocate for those lies. A liar wants to feel supported and justified, knowing what they hide. They do not care about the effects of the lie as long as it does not boomerang back to them as the culprit so that they can blame others. Once exposure sheds light on a lie, the liar faults everyone else and never accounts for their actions. A deceiver finds no purpose in lying if it is not believable.

It reminds me of the "boy who cried wolf," someone who lies so much that when it is time for someone to believe the truth, no one does. Once someone is deemed a liar, everything that they say is second-guessed.

There are many ways to know whether someone is lying, but this will require asking questions. Until you verify what is said, there should be no response or action. As believers, you silence lies; you don't spread what you don't know to be true.

Some people accept a lie knowing it is not true because they do not like the truth, and the lie is more entertaining. Some people's entire life is a lie, and because they have lied for so long, they have to uphold their lies to maintain an image or lifestyle. They are prone to believe a lie because they hold no truth and do not like what is true. God searches the heart of man and knows all truth. For He knows, hears, and sees all things. God will send a strong delusion to those who do not have a love for the truth.

"¹⁰ **and with all unrighteous deception among those who perish, because they did not receive the love of the truth, that they might be saved. ¹¹ And for this reason, God will send them strong delusion, that they should believe the lie,"** 2 Thessalonians 2:10–11

There are consequences for lying, and they directly affect the person who lied and those who agreed with the lie. Accepting a lie is an impartation because you agree with a lie that dominates your life now. You can form a covenant with that lie, and the impact will follow you. You must be aware of what you come into agreement with.

The impacts of a lie cause:

Punishment

Delusion

Stunted progression and blessings

Repetitive cycles

Legal Rights to the Enemy

Restlessness

No peace

Generational curses and sickness

Act of being unsettled

Intended lies trap and curse you, and they welcome deception in your life to ruin it, although your life was peaceful before them. Warning always comes before destruction, and the problem I have seen is that people trust too soon. God has a response for those who lie and do not confess and repent.

"A false witness will not go unpunished, And *he who* speaks lies shall perish." Proverbs 19:9

CHAPTER FOUR

PEOPLE PLAY

CHAPTER 4 – PEOPLE PLAY

Some moments in our lives require our undivided attention and attentiveness to how people move around us. There are many facades people put on to get their way, and they play will in your face. Yes, they play in your face. If you are naive, you will fall for it and ruin your life by entertaining the nonsense of others and supporting destiny killers' motives through the advocation of false information.

People will play on people just like they prey on people. A devious person can sense a vulnerable and tampered mind; that awareness they play on this to get their way and then disconnect from others when they are no longer helpful in accomplishing their goal or mission. These devious people play on time and are very sneaky. They are swift to initiate or plant a seed in someone's mind because they know the importance of deceptive time. I call deceptive time the amount of time someone has to act and deceive before people want clarity. A devious person hopes their plans are intact before people start to question their motives. By the time the deceived start asking questions, the deceiver already received what they wanted and planted the seed in the hearts of the masses to spread it. A devious person knows the essence of time.

I will be discussing the different ways people play. If I unveil how people play, it can prevent you from being deceived by the ones you love, associates, and humanity. There are moments when you can involve yourself in things that are nothing like you thought. The deceive gets tangled in the mess and is left to pick up the pieces after the damage. Self-love is being aware. It is better to be mindful first than to get stuck in a mess because of unawareness. Unfortunately, ignorance is costly and does not excuse the pain.

People will take advantage of a kind heart. As a believer, you are to be kind, but you must be wise. I have seen many open their arms up to the same people who destroyed their lives time and time and time again.

Play Victim

Playing "victim" is a significant form of deception. Many will throw rocks and hide their hands and not provide a valid reason for cause of action. The hidden hand is the action that seems to disappear as their side of the story is shared. In this case, many who play victim act on guilt because they are concerned with how the person they threw rocks at will respond. A person can masterly execute this victimhood image by recruiting people who defend them by sharing their narrative and not the whole truth. If the receptive person is naive, they will quickly run with the narrative and not look back. They repeat the same story and spread it, which causes chaos, confusion, and pack bullying as the story lacks the whole truth. I see it happen often.

These false victims feel accomplished and confident with what they did because they have an army of people supporting their behavior, knowing what was untold. When manipulation works, it becomes an ego stroke to the deceiver, but the fall of manipulation is hard.

For an example of victim playing, say you are on a date with a person who you have a strong interest in, and they share with you that their ex cheated on them and they did nothing to deserve it. In your mind, you start to feel bad for them and look at their ex negatively. You start telling them how awful you feel about what they did to them and how they did not deserve it.

However, they did not share with you that they cheated on their ex first and gave them a disease. Had you known the last bit of truth, your perception of the story would have differed entirely. In this case, the person you are dating is deceiving you and playing the victim, which is a perilous game. Hidden Hands.

Your decision to agree with the person you're dating leaves you vulnerable to error in dealing with their baggage. Pay attention to the story.

Does the story add up?

Play on Liking

Play on liking brings me back to the open-arm example. A person can see your open arms and unconditional love for them and will use it to their advantage, blatantly in your face. They recognize you care for them, will forgive them, and take them back every time, even if it is ruining you. These devious people will play on your liking of them to get what they want out of you.

If you are love-blind, you will fall for the bait, and they will drain you out of everything you have and everything you worked so hard to obtain. They will use you in every way and not feel bad for it. When the resources run out, they will turn on you and forget all the risks you took to help them. They are opportunists.

They are observant of who they can easily lie to and manipulate. Deceivers are mindful of who to run their game on and who will prioritize them before themselves. If you risk your livelihood, future, resources, and opportunities for them, they will take you up on the offer.

Never place everything on the line for someone who would not do the same for you. Someone who loves you would never want you to risk your future by making senseless decisions that put you or your loved ones in jeopardy or in harm's way.

Play on Image

Playing on image is a prevalent form of deception. The world has prioritized stereotypes, agendas, stigmas, and image. Society people will tell you what you should and should not have by a certain age. They tell you how successful you should be, what the beauty standards are, the assets you should have, and how your worth is determined. If you meet the worldly requirements, you are deemed successful and find ways to justify and excuse bad behavior by image.

People will use "worldly acceptance" to their advantage and can deceive many through status. For example, people play on being a family man or family woman, a mother or father, where people will go to the gates to support them more than someone who does not hold that image. They are "living the dream." The kicker is the family man and woman are very wicked, but they hide that image behind their children and will use that family persona to get out of trouble. "Your honor, but I have children." The world will be more compassionate in their actions than that of a single and childless person—society standards.

When you think of someone getting arrested for a crime, they first say, "Officer, I have children at home." That is true, but was that thought about before completing the offense? People will play on the image.

People also play on education and success. Many successful people feel they are above the law and entitled to do as they please. They can get out of particular circumstances due to influence and worldly acceptance. They can easily deceive someone due to what they have rather than what they do.

Think of the celebrities many look up to and desire to be just like them. You do not regard undercover deals and transactions surrounding their success. Due to their image and liking, they can use it to deceive others on how they got their fame. Now, everyone is surprised when the truth is exposed.

You trusted an image more than the facts.

Play on Weakness and Insecurities

The play on weakness and insecurities are forms of deception that can be most hurtful. Imagine opening up to someone out of vulnerability, and they use it against you in a time of rage. They can use that information over your head to get you to do what they ask. You feel indebted to them, primarily how they use it against you. In the same way, they feed your weakness to keep you weak.

For example, drug dealers can use drug addicts to get what they want from them because of the addicts' desire to stay high. The more they are kept high, the less they use their mind and cannot see the value of things compared to drugs. A drug dealer can use a drug addict to connect them with more people with an addiction to control their minds.

This dealer is watchful of their weakness to drugs, so they use that weakness to keep them weak for their advantage.

Play on Money

Socially, people love luxury things: high-end cars, fast money, and success. Instant gratification is accepted worldwide and applauded when you find a quick come-up. People can deceive others based on the amount of money they have because of materialistic influence. People can deceive others to do what they want in exchange for cash or a luxury lifestyle. Bribery happens often in these industries and has been silenced and normalized.

There are no limits to people who have the spirit of greed. Morals and values are out the window for the new purchase of a Bentley truck.

In this case, people's minds are molded to success and money value, not actual value, and they hide information, provide half-truths, and partake in the unfamiliar. People will do almost anything to have a "name" in rooms of opportunity, good or bad. The delusion is surface-leveled.

Conversely, people will use you for your money and use money to use you. That is the power money has on the people. This is how deception creeps in because there is no focus or care on human nature. The focus is money. Many people have lost their lives for the love of money. Robberies gone bad, and the sight of purpose lost. The moment is lost.

People can control the minds of others because the way people play goes unhandled. You don't look any deeper than worldly acceptances. Unfortunately, when someone has an ill mission to accomplish something, they search for a weak mind to prey on and to agree.

A devious person will play. Life is a game to them, and their sincerity is nonexistent.

Do not be discouraged if you are deceived because there is still time to make better decisions and break that barrier of deception. Many people have played in my face and thought I was slow, but I gave it to God in prayer, and He provided me with discernment to bring clarity and direction regarding people and their wicked intentions for me. I have done my share of convincing myself to believe that someone was the person I wanted them to be. You are not alone. I had to accept the truth without modifications and emotional blindness. I have accepted that some people are not good people.

The more you show God you can accept the truth, the more He will give you discernment to reveal people's intent. I have learned not to ignore the signs.

Can you accept the truth if someone used you?

PRAYER FOR DISCERNMENT

Dear Heavenly Father,

I pray for everyone reading this prayer. I thank you for preserving them from the dangers of this world, and your Grace and Mercy are their buckler. When they went astray, you still provided for them. I pray, God as they are on this journey with you, that they see the things that others do not. I pray for their supernatural prophetic awareness of people, places, and things. I pray that they keep their eyes steadfast on you, who will keep them in perfect peace. I pray that you reveal the beginning signs of deception so they don't fall into the traps of ignorance and get stuck. I pray that the Holy Spirit will be their comfort and help during times of trouble.

I pray that they embrace your love and care for them so they don't seek validation or need acceptance from others. I pray that they acknowledge the characters of people and how the enemy uses evil doers for assignment. I pray that they read your word so they can know the truth and they do not believe a lie. I pray that you teach them your ways and help them to remain on their course when things are not easy. I pray that you bless them beyond measure for their decision to walk upright in you and have the courage to stand out from the crowd. I pray that you lighten their load of burden, and may it be exchanged with yours. I pray that they learn to walk with you, talk with you, and know when you are speaking.

I pray when things are not right that, you reveal it to them in any sign of warning they need to take heed to. However, you see fit be it so. I pray that you protect them from seen and unseen, incoming and out coming dangers. I thank you that their life is in your Hands and yours alone. I thank you for blessing them with vision and purpose. I pray that they keep their desires to be obedient to you so that their days will be long and they can live in truth and have a prosperous life. May you bless them and keep them.

In Jesus Name

AMEN

CHAPTER FIVE

MIND CONTROL

CHAPTER 5 – MIND CONTROL

Today, I stand and enter the rooms my anointing has prepared for me. Oh, how lovely is the Lord's Favor toward me? He was thinking of me and chose me as one of the living vessels to wise up His people as my assignment. Never in a million years did I see myself walking in the authority He has given me.

I want everyone reading this book to gain wisdom and learn some key indicators of deception where red flags stand out immediately. The worst thing you can do is ignore the red signs when they are present.

In the mind of someone who is deceptive, the goal is to control the minds of how people think, which gives them power and sparks interest to their liking. People can sense vulnerability, weakness, and fear. With that, there are a few traits a person looks for when they are looking to deceive and it aligns with how they think.

1. A Weak Mind
2. A Delusional Mind
3. Overly Sensitive Mind
4. A Collective Mind

A deceiver will monitor how you deal with situations and study how to communicate with you to find out how you can help them reach their goals. To control the mind of someone alludes to power indirectly because it can convert thoughts and behavior to the liking of the controller. Consider what you view as "breaking news." Nowadays, the news can control how you think and feel about a situation based on your limited information.

People put themselves in a panic with the news instead of doing the research. We must strengthen our minds, thoughts, and ideas while weighing outcomes, scenarios, and benefits. We must process everything and confirm all information. We give room for mass deception when we do not strengthen these areas.

Mass deceit is a way of recruitment because there is power in numbers, which is why many focus on the number of people invested rather than what is right or wrong. But mass recruiting cannot stand against the works of God.

Mass recruiting is an expanded scheme to deceive. I will explain how this can destroy a life if they are not strong enough to withstand that type of opposition, especially when standing up for what is right by them self. The first thing I will share is that mass recruiting against someone or a group is a form of bullying. The goal is to weaken the people or person mentally, emotionally, physically, spiritually, and territorially to the intended goal and satisfaction.

The logic of a deceiver is that if they have people to support their poor choices, it is justified and calculated in numbers and connections. They get people to believe their intentions are pure or even good. People fall for it. Mass recruitment builds up the esteem of weak-minded individuals because they feel supported. No matter how many people support poor and bad decisions, they are never justified and never end well. The bigger the deception, the greater the fall.

Deceivers recruit because it gives them the feeling of authority and power to mass manipulate. They dare not tell what they did because of the fear of judgment and attack. Gossip and slander are forms of mass recruiting; influencing people to say, repeat, and share the gossip with others. Gossip is a fast way to destroy someone's reputation because, in the spirit, it eats away at your mind. The life of an intended gossiper will find themselves with years of suffering and regret.

Mass recruiting is like selling a pitch story at a car dealership. The world has itching ears, and people itch for news. They itch to hear anything without testing it—whatever appeases the flesh, even if it is a lie. What I have learned is that those who would rather be lied to are those who have deep-rooted insecurities because the truth hurts.

People can mass recruit through rumors, influence, confusion, lies, deception, gains, and wanting to belong. Deceivers pressure and bully others to recruit and make an enemy out of those who disagree. The long-lasting effects can cause someone to sink into ruin if they are not rooted in the word of God.

I will share ways to defend yourself against these massive attacks that are set to destroy if not addressed. Deception can ruin careers, families, finances, lifestyles, and destiny, which is why you must not play on the dark side or joke about the damage it causes to others. Some high-figure owners' lives were tarnished because of a lie, and they were not equipped to fight against the massive attack. One person against one thousand lies can be challenging. But greater is He that is within you.

"You are of God, little children, and have overcome them, because He who is in you is greater than he who is in the world." 1 John 4:4

The battle is spiritual, and the weapons of our warfare are not carnal but mighty in the Lord for the pulling down of strongholds. Once you have accepted that it was never about people or the number of people, you can see things for what they are. Where the Lord is present, demonic spirits opposed to God will attack in the flesh. The world you reside in is not your home, and the people in it do not love the God you serve. You won't always understand why people move in pure wickedness, as that is not your heart.

You must pray, fast, seek wisdom and Godly counsel, and be bold as a believer, knowing the God who goes before you in all things. You may have to stand alone in a season when everyone disagrees with you. But you do not live a life to accommodate the world, its acceptances, and validations.

Many live under the will, influence, and mind control of others, and because of this, they never fully understand the full effects of their actions and can never explain their actions without name-dropping someone else. Be mindful of others who make decisions solely based on others' opinions without discerning the spirit yourself. When it is all said and done, and people have the time to reflect on their actions, they are not pleased with their decisions because they act not on their own thinking but the thinking of others. Always remember that people gear conversations, situations, and concerns to liking, image, and control. Deception.

CHAPTER SIX

THE ADVANTAGE

CHAPTER 6 – THE ADVANTAGE

You cannot miss the details. Deception is a deliberate skill to alter how someone feels, thinks, or acts. Anyone who deceives others is willing to live a jeopardized life as the "lifestyle" requires upkeep. Those who mishandle, mistreat, and intentionally misguide others operate under a reprobate mind—a loss of moral reasoning. Reprobate minds are not concerned with what is right, noble, just, honorable, or pleasing in the sight of God. Only the righteousness of God can decontaminate a reprobate mind.

A deceiver sees an advantage in brainwashing others. In their minds, the cost of the action does not compare to the reward of the advantage. When things go wrong, they don't understand the long-term effects of a momentary gain. "No one will ever know."

The first advantage a deceiver sees is the opportunity to keep their hands covered while allowing others to play their front line. When you consider mass deceit, a deceiver has a better chance of hiding their actions if others play a part. The goal is to hide the shameful actions to obtain the outcome they see as beneficial. A mastermind deceiver finds a way to hide their tracks and draw people in to place others at the forefront of their problems while taking no accountability for their actions. If not careful, the consequences of a deceiver will land on the people they deceived.

The advantage they see is playing the back of a fire they started and watching from the sidelines as the fire burns—a way to escape the trouble it caused. The fire destroys many lives, and this continues until someone stands against the deception with truth and waters the fires. You cannot defeat deception with fire against fire.

The second advantage a deceiver sees is a clean reputation and the ability to be impressive in the sight of others. Their reputation matters more than the detriments of their actions. As satan masquerades "like an angel of light," so does a deceiver. Whatever view is needed to get to their end goal is their priority. The advantage is how they present themselves to others when looking to recruit. You will see a person's true colors, ways, and motives when they do not get what they want or you question their actions. The Bible says, "Out of the abundance of the heart, the mouth speaks" (Luke 6:45). Time is the missing factor. It will be as if you do not know the person or never did, which is a disheartening factor of deceit. You never knew their true colors. The stronghold this can have on the deceived is their disbelief in what happened. The deceived cannot fathom the factuality of being lied to and used, so they never address the issue, suppress their emotions, and try to erase the deceit from their memory as if it never happened. When deceit meets light, the deceiver and the deceived want to remove it from their recollections of what happened because of the guilt and shame that lingers with it and not wanting to deal or associate with the problem. A deceiver seeks to control how others view them, so they spend much time trying to brainwash others.

The third advantage a deceiver sees is relevancy. I have come to notice that those who seek attention, constant validation, and people pleasers have experienced traumas that yearn for the desire to be seen and heard. Please do not get me wrong; we all need to be esteemed or affirmed by others sometimes. As people, we should always want to help build up the confidence of others, but it is not our responsibility. A deceiver looks for ways to stay relevant, like those who feed and engage in constant drama to have something to say. When people get desperate to remain relevant, they do things they never would. Similar to publicity stunts. Under this umbrella of relevancy, some would betray, confuse, steal, downplay, deflect, accuse, manipulate, victimize, harm, persuade, and lie. Who would have known a cry for attention would cause so much pain to others? When you are discerning, it is easier to avoid these tricks.

Unfortunately, these tactics work on the vulnerable and the weak in heart because they are gullible enough to absorb anything said without thought. They trust anything without thought. They act on anything without thought. They form opinions without thorough thought. They conclude scenarios without thought. Emotions stay unprocessed. Thoughts stay unprocessed. They eventually become a dumping ground for everyone's problems.

The fourth advantage a deceiver sees is power. The ability to use others to get what they want. The carelessness one must have. Believe it or not, a deceiver places many things on the line based on their choices, whether they see it or not. Although their mindset may be "I have nothing to lose," they lose everything. The fool mentality is that the gain surpasses the possibilities of other outcomes and scenarios. They don't want to relinquish the expectations when they have placed so much passion, time, and effort into a mission. Just like how people become obsessed, they don't want to let go of the effort in the mission. Obsession with love. Obsession to hate.

Think of a goal you are ambitiously focused to accomplish. No matter what anyone says, you have tunnel vision to achieve it. Similar to a deceiver and their efforts. Deceivers premeditate most situations, as they don't happen overnight. I pray that God reveals the hands of man, known and unknown, seen and unseen, and all timelines. You cannot control what others do; you can prepare for it. A deceiver continues their actions because they live in denial and do not want to waste their efforts. During exposure, they direct their attention to the time and effort placed on deception because they do not wish to have a failed mission. Their efforts become more evident than letting the ego go, clouding judgment and reality.

The fifth advantage a deceiver sees is feeling justified even when wrong. Unfortunately, they feel justified and confident if they have enough people to support their destructive behaviors, not realizing there are just more in numbers to see the downfall. There is no telling how far a deceiver will go to pamper their ego. The boost of an ego is destructive for a person who deceives intentionally.

The advantages a deceiver sees are disadvantages, and it takes maturity and wisdom to acknowledge that. What comes up must come down. Deception lasts only for so long, but the deceiver and the deceived are affected.

The armies of mass deception will fall and be destroyed by the power of God. You may not be able to stand against it alone, but you have the power of God that fights for you. To shame, every attack will land, and with your eyes will you see it.

"⁷A thousand may fall at your side, And ten thousand at your right hand; *But* it shall not come near you. ⁸ Only with your eyes shall you look And see the reward of the wicked." Psalm 91:7-8

CHAPTER SEVEN

THE FIGHT AGAINST DECEIT

CHAPTER 7 – THE FIGHT AGAINST DECEIT

⁶ Let no one deceive you with empty words, for because of these things the wrath of God comes upon the sons of disobedience. ⁷ Therefore do not be partakers with them." Ephesians 5:6-7

When you allow deception in, the wrath of God will be present. God wants you to be mindful of the information you take in. People have deceptive mouths, and you cannot take every word for face value. Let no one deceive you; this is an easy door for destruction. You may not always know who is deceiving, but their character will represent them. Wherever evil is around you, God wants you to get from among them. Deception captures the mental and causes spiritual bondage, which manifests in the physical. A deceived person aligns their emotions and thoughts around a word and responds impulsively. Anything that opposes the plan of God is the devil's work. The works of deception are like Goliaths set in your path to destroy, control, and ruin your future. But, as a believer, you have the power, dominion, and authority to dismantle any Goliath meant to frustrate your future. With your Faith, you can destroy the barriers you face with God Almighty's power.

The wicked in spirit love to deceive and operate in no wisdom as their hearts are tainted and compromised. There are no limits to the cruel, and their schemes are never-ending. A deceiver's mouth contains lies, threats, trouble, and evil. Evilness is their playground, but God destroys it all. God blocks the hands of the workers of iniquity and disrupts all of their activities. All of their attacks are put to shame by the Glory of God.

"Vindicate me, O God, And plead my cause against an ungodly nation; Oh, deliver me from the deceitful and unjust man!" Psalm 43:1

When you pray and invite God into your situation, He will respond against the hands of the deceiver, whether it be a friend or a foe, close or far, known or unknown. He will reveal their hands. The Lord will vindicate you from opposing forces' works, putting their time, efforts, plans, and minds together to go against you. The mind is a potent tool and should not go to waste. By your Faith to believe, you are set free.

God wants you to build relationships with Him and desires for you to seek the Kingdom of God first. Growing in intimacy with God will strengthen your ability to withstand because you have Heaven's backing. When I prioritized my relationship with God, He became first in my life above all others. In the process of God's vindicating, He will reveal to you what remains dormant in your heart. Cleansing your heart will equip you to discern others and free you from inner damage. When you do the necessary work to be pure, holy, and honorable in the sight of God, He will gift you the wisdom to test the character and motive of anyone surrounding you. Trust no idle word. When examining the words of others, consider the volume the words hold, the value, and the action alignment with the words said. Pray against the spirit operating in people and identify the root cause of the deception. Read scriptures regarding deception and God's vindication against it and the people and meditate on the scriptures. Ask God to reveal the true character in people.

"You shall destroy those who speak falsehood; The LORD abhors the bloodthirsty and deceitful man." Psalm 5:6

Abhors - regard with disgust and hatred

Trouble comes when you trust empty words that have no value. Word curses, unfulfilled words, words that bring zero light to a situation, words that bring more confusion and no clarity, words intended to harm, destroy, and conceal the truth to bring trouble.

Deception disconnects you from God's will because God opposes deception. After all, it is filled with lies, which He hates. Deception looks like a "friend" willing to betray at any time, a relationship with outside motives, a person who shows fake concerns, and someone looking to prey on vulnerabilities.

A deceiver portrays themselves as a solution solver but intends to cause more problems without a trace. They perfect their outward appearance, persona, and reputation to increase the chances of deception. It becomes easier for them to do at this point. The concern is once a person is under a delusion, they lack accountability and are easily led into ditches because the blind in spirit leads them. God destroys the stronghold and will fight for you against the powers of deception, and you must use wisdom moving forward and not make the same mistakes. Repeated mistakes are no longer mistakes but a choice to walk in error.

The truth is many would be here today had they discerned and harkened to God's voice. Take heed to the warnings and attend to the emotions of your spirit- man. Please do not ignore it and make it into what you want it to be because that becomes self-deception. Further, seek God for clarity and direction. You have the victory in

God, and the battle is from a position of victory as you cannot win in the flesh. When the red flags are there, you do not act against them in your flesh but fight the attack in the spirit by taking it to God. God speaks to your spirit, but you observe in your flesh.

Amen.

CHAPTER EIGHT

AT ITS CORE

CHAPTER 8 – AT ITS CORE

Say you were looking to book a hotel in another state, and you were on a website that showed you two 4-star hotels. The first hotel had better images, pricing, location, and amenities than the second 4-star hotel.

Which hotel would you choose?

Most would say the first hotel because of the information on the website and how it was presented and interpreted. I can compare this booking to the perception of how you see what you see. Your perception can be a blessing or a curse. The way you view circumstances can be developmental or detrimental. When information is shared, you develop your outlook surrounding that information. Some people are one-sided with information, so they conclude their outlook solely based on one side of the story without complete comprehension. This type of person is prone to attract deceivers as their minds are made to believe one side of the story. When a person's mind is made, there is never a good reason to try and persuade them of anything as they look to misunderstand you. Pointless. A deceiver is crafty enough to use a person's common perspective to their advantage.

Going back to the example, imagine checking into the first hotel you deem better, and when you stepped into the hotel, it was nothing like the website. The images, the price, and the environment were all false advertisements. You trusted the website, as you believed it to be a reliable source, and it was not.

- You trusted the website and deemed it to be a reliable source .. wrong

- The price was correct .. wrong

- The location was good .. wrong

- The rooms were like the images .. wrong

The deception was in the source you considered to be credible and reliable, which was the website. Only when you are close and personal can you see it, and it can happen to the wisest. Could this have been prevented? Maybe? Maybe not? Wisdom lessens the chances of deception—picture painting. The website painted this picture of the hotel in your mind, and you took the bait. Like people, they will paint a narrative to favor their objective and reason, and if others embrace it, they will continue.

Your outlook on life, people, things, environments, situations, conversations, and relationships falls under perception. Perception falls into destiny because a disfigured outlook can affect how you see your future.

When I am reflecting on my perception, I ask myself the following questions:

- How am I viewing the situation?

- Am I logically thinking this situation through?

- Did I weigh out all other points of view?

- Are there any actions needed to improve my outlook?

- Does my perception align with the will of God?

- Is my view based on another person's outlook or solely on what I concluded?

- Is this outlook benefiting me?

- How does this perception connect to my future?

- Does my outlook affect others negatively? If so, what can I do to prevent that?

Wisdom tells me to consider my perception, others' perception, and the surrounding and environmental perception.

You don't have to care what someone thinks, but understanding their perception is wisdom. When you are attentive to another person's perception, you can discern whether their perception can affect you in any way.

For example, if someone perceives you as a target. You can discern this by the looks, treatment, and what they say. Key indicators that show not to trust them, and this should tell you that they can prey on you at any moment. You should set boundaries and limit the conversations to what you share. Be mindful of their presence and dealings.

A deceiver also monitors others' perceptions by how they handle the information they share and how they respond to that information. They also monitor the emotions that come with what they say. If a person robs a bank and shares that information with their friend, they will monitor how their friend responds because they want to decipher whether that friend will tell or become an enemy in their disapproval.

How do you have the correct perception?

- Consult with God for clarity

- Check all basis

- Verify all information provided

- Weigh out the pros and cons

- Discern the situation

- Connect the dots

- Find root causes

- Confirm your thoughts are yours

- Talk it out

No clouded judgment. One thing to remember is that anyone willing to alter your perception intentionally is living a compromised lifestyle. Compromised beings thrive in corrupted perception because they feel a step closer to achievement. They are looking for others to do their dirty work.

Say a stranger asked you to help change the battery in their car at night because they were trying to get home. Out of pity, you get your jump cables, flashlight, and tools from the back of your truck. Near a gas station with cameras, you help him change the battery, and he says thank you, starts the car, and leaves. What he does not tell you is that he is stealing the vehicle. Say the owner reports the car missing, and the police investigate.

Did the stranger intentionally or accidentally not provide the information?

Who are the main suspects to the police?

What if the police knock on your door because of the gas station cameras?

By the Grace of God, He vindicates you, but consider the unnecessary stress you caused for yourself and your family. The deception was in what was not said and your pity for their situation—just like that, deceived. I don't know anyone who would voluntarily take on this problem. The stranger knew what he did, and he recruited you to help him steal a car while you thought differently. Your perception showed pity for someone who was a carjacker and took advantage. He corrupted your perception of the situation because he did not tell you the whole truth.

How could you handle this tricky and time-sensitive situation differently?

- **Asked questions:** How long has he had the car, and when did it start giving problems?

- **Phone calls:** Call law enforcement from your car to inform them you are helping a stranger change a battery near the gas station. Provide location. Phone a loved one to advise and text them also for documentation purposes.

These additional steps help you better discern his reaction to your questions and whether it is a good idea to help him. The intent of your heart was kind, but the intent in his heart was wicked. Just because you have the best interests of others does not mean they have the best interests of you. Sorry to disappoint some, but there is no guarantee of the reciprocation of genuineness.

Deception at the core is when someone can deceive you based on what was never said. Based on the information provided caused you to make assumptions and react. Your thoughts and perceptions formed around what was not said. Deceit at a core because this is an easy way for a deceiver to blame shift by your input and response based on insinuation. They can escape accountability in their role with sayings like:

- "Technically, I did not say that."

- "You made that up in your own mind."

- "I shared what I knew."

- "I did not tell you to do that." Played and reversed.

You must discern what is said and what is not. Do not make logic out of something that has no logic. Only until it makes sense do you respond and react. Deception is to withhold information from someone, knowing that the withheld information can change the way someone thinks, feels, understands, and acts in a situation. Control. The withheld information alters the response because it is not morally based on understanding. You are liable for what you do not know because an altered decision does not change the current circumstances and consequences.

CHAPTER NINE

IT IS SPREADING

CHAPTER 9 – IT IS SPREADING

Deception is heavily in the categories of influence:

- Media
- Education
- Finances
- Business
- Health
- Money
- Technology
- Weather and Travel
- Cars
- Housing
- Religion
- Laws
- Music
- Entertainment

Any discussion in these categories will trigger humankind's attention because they matter to the people and can raise deep concerns. Lies and misinformation can spread in these areas of influence, as people are eager to listen and be cognizant.

You must discern any idle words in any category of discussion.

I briefly talked about the need to belong. The urge to belong can corrupt the mind to connect with detrimental communities, people, conversations, and environments. I have noticed this happens when you try to fill a void with people. The desire to just be connected to feel important, heard, and validated.

Deception creeps in those with a void in their heart. Whether the deceived or the deceiver, those who instigate problems want to be seen, heard, and involved. Deceivers know what to say to get people thinking and what talks would make dinner tables.

This generation is damaged, broken, and hurt. From one generation to the next, the hurt of deception will continue until the leading generation, undivided, takes a stand to go against it and shed light, which is the word of God.

I share ways deception can spread among generations of people. The spread is like weeds in the garden that come to destroy the harvest. Deception disrupts your thinking, emotions, character, reputation, progression, efforts, and future. Weeds destroy silently.

Words like curses are like weeds. Some people think words are just words and cannot hurt, but they can if you accept what is untrue and are not walking in your God-given identity. Words from your mouth have been placed in the atmosphere, activating spirits on assignment. When people talk about you, your mind processes the words as true when they are a lie, and people spend years casting down the thoughts. People spread deception by using word curses. When words speak against you, they are word curses and purposed to change the way people view you. If not addressed, it can cause deep depression, lack of confidence, isolation, and suicidal ideations. The enemy is the accuser of the brethren and is constantly looking for reasons to accuse you. Deceivers are always looking for ways to tarnish your image and reputation, to see your life in shambles. It is not bad enough for them to say ill words, but they want to see the damage they have caused with their own eyes. They thrive in damage.

One way people can spread deception is by always wanting to be heard. They never stop talking. They tend to overshare over boundaries, and there are no limits to what they share. It is hard for them to listen as they disregard everything. Their life is filled with disappointments because their own words let them down. The desire for others to listen causes them to be loose at the mouth. Gossipers who speak about others gossip about themselves and do not know it as they do not discern who they share information with. They may have been ignored or disregarded in life and believe this is the moment they have never had. Deception spreads through them because they are a gossiper and will share the news with anyone willing to listen and entertain it. Sometimes, we want others to hear us, but what are we saying, and who are we listening to?

The second way people can spread deception is by wanting to be seen. Attention seeking. "Hey, look at me." They want to be noticed and desire to be the cause of something or live a life to prove a point. They hope to be the news breakers or the first to share information. They do not validate what they share because they are passionate about sharing the news first. They feel needed and esteemed when recognized for the information they discuss. Society people want to go viral and want to gain attention. There is no telling how far they would go for it, to the degree of risking their future, freedom, and even life to prove a point. Deception spreads through them because attention becomes a craving for food, and there are no measures for how far they will go. After gaining attention, they feel accomplished. You can see what type of attention they seek, even by sets of friend groups.

The third way people spread deception is by the desire for inclusivity—the longing to be. There is a yearning for acceptance. The dangers of wrong communities can cause a lifetime of recovery. The wrong relationships, environments, communities, business partners, advice and guidance, and purpose can lead to a lifetime of recovery, and some never return from the damage. Deception spreads through them because there are no limits to what they would do to be accepted, and once accepted, they can give room to deceive others to join them. It reminds me of fraternities and sororities, where people will do rituals just to be included despite the emotional or physical damage and trauma they face because of it. I have seen many come out of these organizations and have the boldness to share their testimony. A deceiver will prey on those who want to be accepted by others.

The fourth way people spread deception is by ignorance and delusion. Most people will spread information incognizant. Confidently defending what they are oblivious to or have little to no evidence to support their view. Deception spreads through them because they are the defenders of ignorance. This spread of deception comes from people who feel entitled because of status, class, and the number of supporters. The damage of ignorance has always been hard for me to see because many are affected and have no rooted understanding of the deception. Some people want to be correct and never want to face their wrongs. The rude awakening is always untimely. Some people have a natural heart to defend, but you must be up to date with what you are protecting. Deception can spread through ignorance defense because people believe they are defending what is right. They let a kind heart fall into ignorance and deception.

To fight this deception:

- Have all the information.

- Ask all the relevant questions.

- Verify all information from steps A to Z.

CHAPTER TEN

TRUTH SEEKER

CHAPTER 10 – TRUTH SEEKER

Where there is truth, darkness is unsettled and cannot remain. You face deception with the truth. As a believer of Christ, you have to love the truth and want the truth to prevail. Darkness cannot stand where there is truth. A truth seeker wants to know the core of information. Most people do not like the truth because they don't want to deal with what the truth comes with. Truth is only through the Lord Jesus Christ.

"Jesus said to him, "I am the way, the truth, and the life. No one comes to the Father except through Me." John 14:6

Many are deceived because the Holy Spirit does not guide them. When you have the comforter to guide you, you can pray for truth in all areas of your life. Some people are ashamed of the truth and want to hide in darkness. When deceivers restrain the truth, there will be bondage because truth is what sets you free. There are reasons why they hide the truth, and you must constantly be discerning. People will fight the truth to prevent it from being exposed. When it is exposed, you will see how darkness triggers and runs.

The world rejects Jesus and His teachings as He is the truth. Until His return, there will always be a battle between good and evil, truth and lies. You will notice when you are a truth carrier, the world will be quick to dismiss you, be offended, and make you an enemy and a target. Because the world hated Christ, so they will also hate you. At times, for no explainable reason at all. The world covers deception, and those who carry a light will stand out. Similar to you going into a store and everyone notices you, in the spirit, opposing spirits can sense your presence in the atmosphere.

The glory of God rests on you, and God sets you apart. Opposing spirits set to attack and provoke you because of God's favor for you. The enemy hates the way that God shields you, comforts you, blesses you, and uses you to defeat and expose the kingdom of darkness. Deception cannot rule where there is truth to destroy the works. You know the truth because of the word and knowledge of God. You speak out against deception with the word of God.

"Certainly not! Indeed, let God be true but every man a liar. As it is written:

"That You may be justified in Your words, And may overcome when You are judged." Romans 3:4

I will share how to detect a lie and discern what is true.

1. Everything that is said should align with the word of God. Discern what goes against kingdom principles, things that are pure, holy, and just. Discern what goes against the Fruit of the Spirit. Discern what moves you away from the promises of God.

2. Prayer changes things. Pray and ask God for confirmation, clarity, revelation, discernment, and guidance on how to address situations.

3. Wait for God's response. Do not act on what anyone says until God provides confirmation. Process all thoughts and emotions. Do not act, respond, or defend a word with a temporary emotion. Deception creeps in without understanding.

4. Test everyone's spirit. Reread chapter 1, The Sprout. Test every person, friend group, and engagement and compare what they say to their character.

5. Consider different motives and why they shared the information with you. Did they expect how the information would make you feel, respond, and act? What is the intent?

6. Consider the core. Everything has a core and a purpose. "It was for no reason" is a lie. Where is the word rooted? Get the beginning of the knowledge.

7. Truth seekers ask questions. If information is not clear, do not be afraid to ask questions. Unasked questions become assumptions and lead to deception. Assumptions are not facts.

These steps can prevent slander, gossip, and deception from spreading. Truth seekers must be mindful of information that is regurgitated and repeated. Wisdom is to seek truth in all things that oppose God's will and word. Truth seekers come with a boldness from God to expose lies, destroy the works of deception, and defend what is right. Although people may invite you into their issues, be absent. You do not need to entertain everything. When God gifts you with discernment, you can see right through people. You need discernment to deal with today's world because there is a pull for chaos.

PRAYERS FOR TRUTH SEEKERS AND CARRIERS

Dear Heavenly Father,

I pray for everyone reading this; I ask that you strengthen them and give them the boldness to fulfill their assignment. I pray that they stand for truth against the rulers of darkness and the principalities that try to silence their voices. God, I ask that you give them wisdom to see what lies before them. Open their eyes so that they may see, and open their ears so they may hear. I pray that the Holy Spirit guides them into all truth and vindicates them from those who try to destroy their character, lies, false narratives, and all forms of deception. I pray against these attacks, and the yokes of them be destroyed by the blood of Jesus. May they carry the truth with courageousness despite who comes against it. I pray that you bless their voice and give them the wisdom to use discretion. I pray they see the light within them, and they do not dim it for anybody. May they walk in truth in all things. The God who responds by fire may you light up their path with your glory, grace, and mercy that sustains and is their shield from works of evil.

May they accept what people show them and not justify character with emotion. I pray they are truth seekers and truth carriers forever to speak the word of God relentlessly. I ask that you preserve them as they go through life.

In Jesus Name
AMEN

CHAPTER ELEVEN

I UNDERSTAND

CHAPTER 11 – I UNDERSTAND

I previously had a workshop about the importance of walking in wisdom. Truth defeats deception, and wisdom provides insight into the difference between a truth and a lie. There are different components to walking in wisdom. God gives wisdom to those who ask. If you desire wisdom, God will grant it. Wisdom prevents, protects, and guides us through life. When you have wisdom, it is harder for liars to lie to you. The benefits of wisdom are everlasting. Wisdom can save you from fixing mistakes and errors and requires you to seek God before everything.

The Fear of the Lord is the beginning of wisdom.

Fear of the Lord

"The fear of the LORD *is* the beginning of knowledge, But fools despise wisdom and instruction" Proverbs 1:7

The Fear of God is giving reverence and honor to God. You will have so much peace when you welcome God into your daily life and every activity. You consider God in all that you do. You care what God thinks, and with such honor for Him, you do not want to disappoint. You care about God's perspective and pray that you view things like He does. You are concerned with what God says and is doing through you, His direction, and His perfect Will.

You honor God's presence and continually give thanks for what He has done. The Fear of God is removing all idols. Anything can become an idol: relationships, money, success, family, celebrities, and wealth. God comes first. You bring to your remembrance all God has done.

You consult with God about everything.

- You have to know what to do
- You have to know what to say
- You have to know where to live
- You have to know who to marry
- You have to know how to move
- You have to know when to speak
- You have to know when to be silent
- You have to know when to start a business
- You have to know what church to attend
- You have to know who to believe
- You have to know who to connect with

- You have to know how to handle problems. The Fear of the Lord gives access to the King of Glory, who gives insight to those who seek Him. God knows the end from the beginning. God is the only one who knows everything, sees everything, and hears everything. Omnipresent is He. God responds to you from a place of being all-knowing.

Now, fools despise wisdom. Deceivers do not operate in wisdom; they operate in carnality, believing they control all outcomes. They think they are their own god. Lowercase g.

Knowledge

The Fear of the Lord is the beginning of knowledge. Once there is reverence for God, you consider Him in all you do and acknowledge that you do not own your life. He will reveal to you the knowledge of God, trusting that you will use that knowledge as He sees fit. He will reveal those things you do not know in a way you will understand. God will provide you with knowledge and heighten your spiritual gifts for the journey. (1 Corinthians 12:4-11).

The Spiritual Gifts are:

- Gifts of Wisdom
- Gifts of Knowledge
- Gifts of Faith
- Gifts of Healing
- Gifts of Miracles
- Gifts of Prophecy
- Gifts of Discerning of Spirits
- Gifts of Different Kinds of Tongues

- Gifts of Interpretation of Tongues

Knowledge is essential and will help you not take wrongdoings personally. When you seek God, He provides you with knowledge. Knowledge can reveal hindsight, insight, and foresight. Many are destroyed because of a lack of knowledge, and when knowledge is rejected, God will also reject you and your children.

"My people are destroyed for lack of knowledge. Because you have rejected knowledge, I also will reject you from being priest for Me; Because you have forgotten the law of your God, I also will forget your children." Hosea 4:6

Take heed to the knowledge of God and all of His righteousness. You can obtain knowledge with intimacy with God.

Understanding

With knowledge comes understanding and revelation. You must decipher what to do with the knowledge. Understanding brings clarity. You need understanding before making decisions. To your spirit by the Spirit of God. When God provides understanding, He downloads it into your spirit, man. God can reveal what you can expect in a move of God and during your breakthrough. The Lord of the Breakthrough is in control. You will know in parts.

"For we know in part and we prophesy in part."

1 Corinthians 13:9

Get Understanding.

Instruction

God gives instructions. As a believer, when you are in the Will of God. He will lead and provide you with instruction, just as He instructed Moses, Joshua, David, Jeremiah, and many others in the Bible. The task may look impossible, challenging, scary, and not make sense to our carnal mind, but it is what God requires. Instructions from God will protect you from the effects of deception. God will provide you a way of escape from the traumas of deception.

Divine direction is wisdom because you have more knowledge than earthly understanding. If God is pulling you away from or directing you to a person, place, or thing, there is reason. You must listen. You will find obedience to the Lord to be good.

"He who heeds the word wisely will find good, And whoever trusts in the LORD, happy *is* he." Proverbs 16:20

Obedience

Not only do you hear the instructions of God, but you do it. When you consider your plans vs God's plan, obedience is not always the easiest or your first option. Obedience requires shedding your carnal and fleshy desire and letting go of your expectations of how your life will turn out to align yourself with what God has for you. You do not always understand, but God is a protector and will cover you as you fulfill your purpose. The enemy sends chaos to disrupt your assignment and to cause confusion. But God is faithful, and disobedience is costly.

When you are outside the will of God, there is no protection. Disobedience will cost you time, blessings, happiness, health, freedom, joy, and peace. Deception can cost you all of these things as well. Deception brings ruin. You shield yourself from the attacks of deception in obedience to God.

> "But be doers of the word, and not hearers only, deceiving yourselves." James 1:22

Correction

People do not turn from their deception because of pride, arrogance, entitlement, rebellion, and idolatry. Whether they are the deceiver or the deceived, God will send correction. The correction of God is His love to stop the tracks of destruction.

> "He who disdains instruction despises his own soul, But he who heeds rebuke gets understanding." Proverbs 15:32

Taking heed to correction is wisdom. Correction is what shapes and builds your character for the kingdom of God. Blessed is the one who keeps God's commands, order, and judgments.

God corrects with a warning.

The warning comes before destruction. God warns against doing, listening to, or acting on anything against His Will to prevent the unseeable and the foreseeable. Anything that takes place on Earth has already taken place in the Heavens.

God corrects with conviction.

God will place knowledge in your spirit to stop a habit, an action, or a plan, and you will feel a pull on your heart that something is wrong. There is a desire to change ways or direction. God can even convict you as a destiny helper to someone else's destiny. The conviction of God may come with restlessness until you walk in obedience.

God corrects with rebuke.

The wrath of God is God's righteous judgment of sin. God has a way of responding to the wickedness and waywardness of the world. His rebuke can be a punishment to realign to God's will. Prideful people do not learn without punishment and consequences; this is the awakening to get their lives in order. God punishes in love. The Lord desires that all come to repentance and not perish.

"The Lord is not slack concerning *His* promise, as some count slackness, but is longsuffering toward us, not willing that any should perish but that all should come to repentance." 2 Peter 3:9

Counsel

God's counsel is the revelation of His purpose and plans for you—how He communicates His plans for you. Wisdom is understanding God's purpose for your life, including assignments, plans, and vision. Deception disengages you from God's purpose because God is truth.

When you understand what God is doing and what He requires, you are not easily moved by what the world is doing. The Lord's counsel is what stands when all else fails.

You should connect with like-minded people who understand where you are going and not only where you have been. You should speak with those who give you good, Godly advice and build their foundation on the Lord, our Strong Tower.

Discretion

Discretion will protect you. I have three words to say regarding discretion.

Samson and Delilah.

You must not release a word until God approves it. People prey on weaknesses and opportunities. Discretion is protection.

Discretion is prevention. Discretion will preserve you. Discretion is wisdom. People will wait to destroy everything you worked so hard to obtain. They wait for the moment to make their move against you. Delilah not only used what Samson said against him, but she shared it amongst the Philistines who preyed on his downfall, and they prepared a celebration for his defeat.

Silence against plots is sometimes the best answer. There will come a time to share your story. If someone has lied about you, it is hard not to want to spend your energy defending your name and character, so much so that it takes a toll on you. I would encourage anyone facing an assassination of character to speak the word of God until He vindicates you with His word. Never silence your voice, saying the word of God because that is where your breakthrough comes from.

In addition, there is no need to respond to the actions of others. God will contend with those who contend against you. You will have your day. Vindication is coming! There is a time for everything under Heaven, and you must use wisdom.

Be careful not to overshare. Some blessings are just for your ears. Samson was anointed by God and trusted the wrong person. Delilah was deceptive. When you overshare, someone can deceive you out of your blessings by misleading you in other directions and removing you from God's will.

Discernment

Discernment comes in many ways. The revelation of discernment looks different for all experiences in life. No two walks of life look exactly the same. What did God say? God speaks in many ways:

- Warning (preparation and correction)
- Visions
- Word of God
- Repetitive conversations
- Sermons
- Prophecy
- Prophetic sounds and numbers
- Dreams
- God's Voice
- People
- Experiences
- Memory
- His creation

You can discern others through observation, where you analyze what they say and do. I have formulated questions that I ask myself when I am discerning others. Discernment requires reflecting and processing. Here are some questions I ask myself when discerning others:

- What do they say? (Literally)
- How do they express themselves?
- How do they view other people's successes?

- How do they treat people they do not need?

- What life do they create for themselves? (Trouble, Life, Freedom, Change, Opportunities)

- What is not being said? (Observation, Body language, Eye Movement and Contact, Involvements, Participation)

- What brings them enjoyment?

- Where is their attention and priority?

Reread Chapter 4 to know how people play. Discernment is necessary to prevail in today's time. Different facades and personas mask deceivers. These false personas lead to mass deception in the hearts and minds of people. Until you recognize where to place people in your life:

- Clarify with God

- Gain understanding

- Don't overshare

- Don't be too open and vulnerable

- Don't trust from the gate

- Remain guarded

- Strengthen your discernment

- Pray and ask for wisdom

CHAPTER TWELVE

SELF DECEPTION

CHAPTER 12 – SELF-DECEPTION

It is one thing when people deceive you, but another when you deceive yourself. This chapter will require self-evaluation to look inwardly to see if you are self-deceived. The Bible says that your heart is deceitfully wicked above all else (Jeremiah 17:9 - **"The heart *is* deceitful above all *things,* And desperately wicked; Who can know it?"**). You do not always know the deception in your heart. Without cutting off the surrounding unclean layers of your heart, you are deceived and unaware. You may not have ill motives but if you lack the truth and knowledge of holiness and purity you are in deception. You are in deception if you have an unclean residue of sin, trauma, and pain lying dormant in your heart. A pure heart and clean hands are what God desires.

Trauma, bitterness, resentment, and the enemy's lies may live in the crevices of your heart. There are many spiritual heart conditions; if God has not filtered out the heart, kind words can deceive. Emotion-based responses are deception because your feelings change and are unreliable. Your perception is based on how you feel and not actuality. This type of deception can seep in easily because we all have emotions and empathize with the feelings of others. Your own emotions deceive you.

During my prayer time, I had to seek God because it was hard to understand how people live in deception. He revealed to me that the delusion of others starts with self-deception first. He brought me to 1 John 1:8 – **"If we say that we have no sin, we deceive ourselves, and the truth is not in us."** Many people live a life of denial, so they are self-deceived. Pride. They see no wrong in their actions and become numb to their flaws and faults. Because of this, they are unaware of the changes in times and seasons. Their stubbornness calls them to remain the same and become unprepared for change.

For example, a prideful person would refuse to put on a car seatbelt just because someone asked them to and is in disbelief that they need it as a defensive response. The pride deceives them from seeing any incoming danger, like a car accident, in their refusal to be corrected. They only see and accept the illusion they create and are not realistic. God forbid a car accident happens; their lack of accountability will cause a response like "You jinxed me." Some people stick to their ways.

They are self-deceived to 1. think they don't need a seatbelt and 2. they fault the person who correct them.

I will share the different forms of self-deception as I find them essential to explain.

SELF-SABOTAGE

Self-sabotage looks different for everyone. God plans to prosper you, and self-sabotage opposes this plan and places you on the path of destruction. Tell me you are self-sabotaging without telling me you are self-sabotaging. Low self-esteem, negativity, gossip and slander, easily offended, and lack of ambition are signs of self-sabotage. The deception in self-sabotage is to believe that you are not good enough, which is a lie. So, you give up and become careless and reckless in your actions.

Self-sabotage lessens your interest to accomplish things, and you stand in your own way. Opposing forces will try and stand in the way, but for it to be you to cause your own destruction is deceptive. The outcome of this self-deception is noticeable, and people become what they say.

OVEREXCITEMENT

Overexcitement can cause self-deception because the thought of receiving can outweigh the logic of consequence and responsibility. For example, say your credit score is finally over 700, and you have always wanted to buy a house. Your eagerness to buy a house causes you to accept a loan offer to purchase one. Now, a year in, you are overwhelmed with debt and realize you did not plan effectively to balance your funding for the purchase.

The deception formed from your overexcitement because it looked like a good idea, but it was not without a thorough plan. Feeling overexcited is a happy emotion, but decisions should never form from it alone.

The eagerness to learn from others also gives way to accepting deceptive teaching. The Bible says there will be false prophets that rise in these times. The overexcitement for a prophecy causes you to believe what is not foretelling. You must know God for yourself so your excitement does not ignore the Lord when He speaks. Prophecy should come as a confirmation of what you already know. If what a prophet says or teachings go against the word of God, decline it. Cast down all deception. Do not allow anyone to re-word the scriptures to the liking of the flesh.

"Then many false prophets will rise up and deceive many. " Matthew 24:11

The overexcitement of the flesh includes lust. Lust is when you are seduced by the appearance of another person's looks, and it blinds you from seeing the true nature and character of the person. Lust causes an emotional attachment to the appearance of someone opposed to their values. Some fall in love because of looks and not substance. The self-deception in this is that because of lust, it is easy to take advantage as the true colors are not so apparent, although in plain sight. The strong desire to lust outweighs what is visibly shown.

IGNORANCE

Think about a chessboard and how a pawn protects the king. The disadvantage of a pawn is that depending on you play the board game a pawn can only take one step at a time, and there is more leverage for other chess pieces to remove a pawn off the board and attack from different angles. A pawn is the position of a person in ignorance because you never see the true threat on the board, and you are sometimes sacrificed for advancements.

Think of the story between David and Uriah. David did an awful thing in front of the sight of the Lord by coveting Uriah's wife and impregnating her. David wanted Uriah to sleep with his wife so David could hide his disgrace and cover his sins, but Uriah refused as he wanted to stay loyal to the army. David schemed to have Uriah un-alive by setting him up to be positioned in the front of a battle and advising others not to come to his defense during the war and to back down during the attack. Uriah passed away because of David's setup, and David married his wife. This story exemplifies how Uriah was a pawn because of David's desire to cover his sin and shame.

He deceived Uriah to go to war while knowing his ultimate plan. God saw what he did, and because he committed the sin in private and wanted to keep it hidden, God said He would punish Him publicly.

"⁹Why have you despised the commandment of the LORD, to do evil in His sight? You have killed Uriah the Hittite with the sword; you have taken his wife *to be* your wife, and have killed him with the sword of the people of Ammon. ¹⁰ Now therefore, the sword shall never depart from your house, because you have despised Me, and have taken the wife of Uriah the Hittite to be your wife.' ¹¹ Thus says the LORD: 'Behold, I will raise up adversity against you from your own house; and I will take your wives before your eyes and give *them* to your neighbor, and he shall lie with your wives in the sight of this sun. ¹² For you did *it* secretly, but I will do this thing before all Israel, before the sun.'" 2 Samuel 12:9-12

Although David was called by God, he suffered greatly because of this sin. Uriah was deceived, and his ignorance cost him.

Ignorance is a form of self-deception because you absorb and act on information without comprehension, leaving you vulnerable when more information unravels. Ignorance makes you the doer of your own destruction because you did not seek truth, and you responded. You chose to react to what you did not know. Indeed, you do not know what you do not know, but it is never good practice to act without wisdom. It is no one else's fault when you decide to act impulsively. You can feel hopeless in this position of a pawn, but there is hope for a turnaround. On the chessboard, if a pawn strategically gets to the other side of the board, it can become a queen with more accessibility and range to defend the king. In perspective, the turnaround happens when you seek truth and wisdom without impulsive behaviors. The change starts in you.

As a pawn, what king are you defending?

PITY

The self-deception of pity. People will categorize empathy and pity in the same way. When you have empathy, you can understand the feelings of others, but with pity, you feel sorrow for the suffering and misfortunes of others. You can become self-deceived by pitying others' problems because your emotions make you believe that they do not deserve what they are going through, and you are quick to aid their needs and are insensible to their motives. Pity can prevent you from seeing the potential betrayal and setup. Do not pity others; instead, rationalize what is really going on.

The acts of pity can cause you to end up in the same situation as them when all you want to do is help. Be mindful of those looking for a sob story to captivate the emotions of others. Do not allow your feelings to deceive you into the traps.

EMOTIONAL BLINDNESS

The self-deception of emotional blindness. Love, love, love and more love. The love of others will close your eyes to the red flags they show you. When red flags are ignored and dismissed, they worsen with time. By the time you examine their actions, after being silent for so long, their behaviors are more complex to tame and will cause more significant destruction.

A person's true character, personality, morals, and conduct remain under your nose because of your love for them and the idea of their potential in who they can become. Falling in love with a person's potential is one of the biggest mistakes because they may never change. God wants you to love others and use wisdom in your dealings with people. People will disappoint you.

The love for others should never cause you to ignore the red flags presented. At a minimum, you must acknowledge them because this self-deception trains you to believe someone is one way when they show you another.

For example, in domestic violent relationships, many go back because of emotional blindness and pity. These forms of self-deception cause someone to stay in unhealthy and, at times, fatal situations because of the high hopes of them changing and feeling bad for them.

OBSESSION

The self-deception of obsession with others and what they have. Obsession is a very dangerous characteristic because the mind is trained to want to know or pry information about the life of another person, including those they do not know personally. The urge to have access to them weirdly increases, and some either want proximity to the person, to be the person, or to be with the person. It becomes a desire to control that person, whether physically, emotionally, or mentally, while envying what they have to the degree that they think about the person daily and cannot focus on their own life. They cannot eat, drink, or sleep without that person in their mind. The self-deception in this is to believe that the life they obsess over matters more or is more valuable than their own, which creates an environment of jealousy and they are convinced they deserve what someone else worked hard to obtain. Some go the distance to try to destroy a life they do not know or try to make someone love them to the point where they would risk their own life trying to obsess over the decisions of others and their belongings.

PRIDE

The self-deception in pride. "The know-it-all." "Then I won't stop until I get my way." "The hard-headed." Prideful people believe they know everything and are not open to being corrected, so the problems they face are preventable, but they become delusional when the problems surface. I do not try to explain myself to a prideful person because they will interpret what is said to their preference. The self-deception in pride is that prideful people change narratives to their stance and dilute truth and understanding. The destruction of a prideful person comes as ignorance to them because they do not listen. They boast in their own energy, which later becomes one of their biggest downfalls.

God opposes the proud.

FEAR

The self-deception of fear. This form of self-deception causes you to see things that are not even there. Your worry concludes how you feel your future will be, and you respond out of fear. Fear of the future. Fear of exposure. Fear of people.

Fear of failure. Fear of lack. Fear of non-acceptance. Fear of response. Fear of aftermath.

"For God has not given us a spirit of fear, but of power and of love and of a sound mind." 2 Timothy 1:7

Fear will stagnate you and cause psychological bondage in your mind that immobilizes you from progressing. It also causes you to speak out of fear, think out of fear, and position your life out of fear. You must remember that God is in control of your life and has final authority over what happens to you.

Self-deception causes self-destruction.

Here is my recommendation for those who live in fear: Understand the authority you have to create and speak life over situations. God has given you the power so you can destroy fear by speaking life and life more abundantly. Fear is a mind battle that some people never win, but when you speak life over yourself, your mind has no other option but for your thoughts to align with what you say. God is the only one who holds tomorrow. Man, do not hold your tomorrow, so when you live in fear, you deceive yourself into thinking you know the entire outcome of tomorrow, and you do not. Your life can drastically change in a day, in a blink of an eye, for the better. God will reveal tomorrow to those whom He chooses to share it with, like prophets. He is a God of Grace and Mercy. You should never fear a thing. Destroy the spirit of fear with your words. Do not self-deceive yourself out of a better tomorrow because of the fears of today.

All forms of self-deception are dangerous because they involve believing what is not true and what is not there, overlooking the presented signs of a person, place, or thing, or thinking you are an exception and that it cannot happen to you.

CHAPTER THIRTEEN

SECURITY

CHAPTER 13 – SECURITY

The blood of Jesus Christ defeats deception and will not reign in your life, family, and destiny. The yoke of deception is broken and destroyed with the knowledge of God. You are a new creation in Christ and obtain identity in Him. After repentance of your sins and believing in the burial and resurrection of Jesus Christ, the new has come. The old is gone and washed away by the blood of the lamb. Jesus defeated Hell, death, and the grave so that you may have salvation through Him who believe.

"Therefore, if anyone *is* in Christ, *he is* a new creation; old things have passed away; behold, all things have become new." 2 Corinthians 5:17

In your new identity, the Lord will give you knowledge, boldness, and the urge to seek, speak, and identify truth, including truth in your identity in Him, who created you and knew you before you were formed. When you understand your God-given identity, you can discern those who do not walk in a God-given identity. Everyone will obtain the fruits of their labor. Where and how you labor is what you will produce. The works of your own hands. The laborers of the wicked. The laborers of the good. The laborers will all produce fruits.

When you become and act on the Fruit of the Spirit, you can discern those who do not operate with them. You can easily discern others' energy, activity, and motion as a laborer of good deeds. When you become an act of kindness, you should be able to discern those who are not in kindness by your discipline, awareness, and focus. We live in a world filled with distractions, and we can become easily distracted on our assignments because of people. With your God-given identity, which is God revealing who you are in Him, He will reveal what needs to change. You are now a part of the body of Christ, so you will receive the inheritance of the Kingdom— protection, awareness, and prosperity.

God reveals. God protects. God provides. God responds. God blesses. God speaks. God preserves.

What does a walk with God look like as a new creation in Christ?

1. Place God first, giving reverence to Him and removing all idols.

2. When God speaks. Respond. Listen to what He says, as His plans are never to harm you. For example, God can tell you to remove a friendship that does not serve a purpose during your walk. As hurtful as this may be, God knows best, and you do not see what goes on behind closed doors. You may not understand now, but your obedience in removing that friendship will bring a direct path to you.

3. Build intimacy with God by reading the word of God, Praying, Worshipping, Thanksgiving, and Fasting. You You remain hidden in God's secret place by prayer and supplication to the Lord.

"He who dwells in the secret place of the Most High Shall abide under the shadow of the Almighty." Psalm 91:1

4. Encourage yourself in the Lord like David. Encourage yourself in the word of God. There is a keyword in the prior sentence: yourself. You must speak those things that God says and speak against what He did not say—casting all imaginations down that oppose the knowledge of God.

Your walk with God will reveal to you who you are in Christ. God will reveal newfound passions, purpose, direction, assignment, and the will of God for you. The beauty of living with purpose is that freedom comes to you, and you are no longer bound by society and deception because you have found reason for life. The burdens of your past are not to be carried by you anymore. You can exchange your burdens with the Lord and give your past to Him. The burdens you hold are a choice, as there is no condemnation in Christ Jesus. You can let them go and live a life of peace and order.

5. Live a life of repentance. Repent daily for yourself, your bloodline, and the generations that have not come yet and have gone. Covering all sins under the blood of Jesus. There may be sins that remain unrepented. God is a covenant-making and covenant-keeping God. You are living in an existing prayer, whether the prayer came from you or someone said a prayer for you. Your prayers create covenants with God and the covering of your bloodline.

6. Forgive yourself and others for what they have done. If you have experienced the damage of deception and your heart was pure, forgive them. For God to forgive you, you must forgive them. Forgiveness is not an emotion but a choice. Your feelings will later follow after your decision. Man looks at the outer appearance, but God searches the heart.

Do not hold yourself in the bondage of captivity because of unforgiveness. Forgive yourself once you forgive them, which is not always easy. Everyone has made mistakes, but it is essential to learn from them and gain wisdom to prevent a life of regret. Give yourself Grace.

7. Protect yourself from others and the access you give them to you. Set necessary boundaries. When you open yourself up to others who should not be there, you become uncovered and an open target to attacks, bad advice, and other people's problems. God will send you like kind and destiny helpers to help you along your journey. You will not always feel alone. God calls and assigns people to be there for you and help raise up the Saints of God.

8. Accept the Love of God. While you were still a sinner, Christ died for you. He loves you more than anything on this Earth and calls you His own. You belong to the Lord. The enemy cannot have a way with your destiny because God Almighty stands in the way against it.

"[38] For I am persuaded that neither death nor life, nor angels nor principalities nor powers, nor things present nor things to come, [39] nor height nor depth, nor any other created thing, shall be able to separate us from the love of God which is in Christ Jesus our Lord." Romans 8: 38-39

9. Live a life of humility and accountability. Acknowledge the faults and wrongdoings done to others and do better. There must be a refusal to stay the same and a daily striving to be more like Christ. Remain humble. God blesses the humble. Live a life of servitude to help others move towards destiny. God opposes the proud. Even when you can proudly prove others wrong after constantly being attacked with false

narratives, God wants you to remain humble, and He will respond. The moment you walk in pride, He will remove his hand from the situation and give you over to your own free will. We all do not want that. After God vindicates you from the mistreatment, the victory belongs to Him. Humility is required even when you are right.

When you experience an authentic encounter with God, you have no desire to remain the same. May your walk with God be blessed and your expectations be exceeded.

REPENTANCE PRAYER

Dear Heavenly Father who art in Heaven,

I come before you to lay everything at the altar. I ask for repentance of my sins, and everything I have done that was not pleasing in your sight. I believe you died, and you resurrected on the 3rd day for my sins. I ask that you come into the crevices of my heart and reveal to me what lies dormant. I remove myself from all attachments and engagements, which disconnects me from you. I repent for my sins [name all sins] which are known and any sins unknown. God, I plead the blood of Jesus over my life, and I ask that you carry me through. Today, I exchange my burdens with yours. I thank you for receiving me and placing my sins into the sea of forgetfulness through the new covenant of the Blood of Jesus Christ.

The Bible declares that you remember my sins no more, so thank you for my identity in you. I align my life with the Will of God from this day forward and will live a lifestyle pleasing to you. Help and strengthen me to complete this and remove anyone who is opposed to this journey I am on with you. I forgive those who have hurt me, and I give them over to you. I will not live a life of resentment to anyone but will remain in joy because you set me free. I renounce and denounce any agreements and covenants formed, known and unknown, that go against your Word. I give you the praise, glory, and honor for the rest of my days. I thank you, Lord, for the freedom I have in you. I will share the good news and we will not be silenced or ashamed as you have been gracious towards us. I thank you for the plans that you have for me, and I will be obedient to you.

I thank you for your forgiveness.

In Jesus Name,

AMEN

CHAPTER FOURTEEN

STAND ON IT

CHAPTER 14 – STAND ON IT

Can you stand on the word of God today and hold Him to His word?

When you don't stand for something, you will fall for anything. When defeating the acts of deception, you stand on truth. Being anchored in God causes you to be unwavering and unshakable when change comes and trouble tries to find you. Deception comes to an end when the warrior inside of you rises.

Speak out. Speak up. Speak for. Speak against. Speak about, Speak through. Speak despite. Speak the word of God.

The enemy wants to remove your voice because he apprehends the light in you. There is knowledge in you that the world needs to adhere to for their deliverance from hidden powers and dark entities looking to control. Do not fall for the bait of silence. A nation is deceived. A nation is spiritually oppressed. A nation is impoverished. A nation needs God. And the Lord is using you.

The enemy will have tactics to come against you, and he sends a compromised person to do it. Be not deceived. There will come challenges during your walk with God, and they will require you to stand up. When you are being used to destroy the intent and acts of deception, some may not get it. People may not see what you see, so when God clothes you in confidence and boldness, remember that Heaven's backing you up. It may take years for people to know what you see or have an experience to see it. But that should never stop your assignment because God calls you. Do not allow people who did not create you to destroy your destiny.

Deep deception runs generationally: generational lies, mind control, misfortunes, and poverty. It takes one person anchored in the word of God to stand in the gap against deep deception and destroy the stronghold of the generation. God will then convict the hearts of many and open the eyes of many to fight with them.

Are you the one?

Do you have the Faith to believe?

Do you have the wisdom to speak up and out?

Do you stand for what is holy, just, and honorable, even with opposition?

If the one is reading this, the Lord will have His angels to cover you and your ways.

Spiritual opposition becomes a challenge when you take a stand against deception from those who are already deceived or operate in demonic power. People will have an urge or need to come against you and try to tarnish your image. In the spirit, the enemy does this to weaken your credibility and influence so when speaking God's word people don't believe you when you talk. Spiritual opposition looks like limited resources, closedoff opportunities, sickness, accidents, division, fear, hatred, accusations, blame, and untimely disappointments and grief. But no weapons formed prospers. The world makes good, evil, and evil, good.

> **"Woe to those who call evil good, and good evil; Who put darkness for light, and light for darkness; Who put bitter for sweet, and sweet for bitter!" Isaiah 5:20**

When you expose the hidden tactics of the enemy, he is the accuser of the brethren, so he would try to use people to deem you foolish, unequipped, unknowledgeable, crazy, and problematic. But God already told you and revealed to you the hidden things. Do not allow people and society to confuse you with what you know. You have to stand.

Another tactic the enemy uses is to make you feel like it is all in your head. When you know what you know and you see what you see. It is a lie of deception used to confuse; do not believe it. Take heed to wisdom. Many people would be here today if they had listened to that gut feeling and God's warning. When you labor in the plans of God, you will produce good fruits generationally. Remember that your decision to live upright covers a generation under God. So, do not quit, and do not throw in the towel.

The world hates you anyway. There will come challenges far worse than the world prepares for. Endure to the end. Despite all you will endure, God sends His peace with you. You will have trouble, but the Lord will keep and deliver you from them all. Great power and authority come in boldness. People are consumed with tales and stories accommodating to the flesh, but God is raising a remnant of people who are unafraid to speak the truth.

Where He leads you to, He brings you through. And that settles it. Shout it from the mountaintop if you have to.

CHAPTER FIFTHTEEN

WE CONCLUDE

CHAPTER 15 – WE CONCLUDE

Thank you for taking the time to get this far in this book. May God bless you and keep you. With the knowledge and gems I share, the enemy is upset because His tactics will no longer work on you and won't shame you. You are ending cycles and destroying yokes. You are standing in the gaps against deception and all other works of the wicked.

Remember to stay in the lane God sends you to as you continue to fight the good fight. God prepares and equips those for the battles you are to fight. Some people face unnecessary battles and warfare because they insert themselves where God did not place them. Stay in your God-given Lane because there lies security and guidance from Heaven.

Cycles break today. Silence breaks today. Immaturity breaks today. Curses break today. Deception breaks today.

Everyone should not have access to you, and with the knowledge you obtain. Please set the necessary boundaries when it comes to people. There will be people who come into your life and are so intrigued that they feel obligated to get close to you. Here, you must use discernment to know who you give entry to and who to leave at the door. Protecting your peace, sanity, and self-control should be a priority, so if there are any interruptions to this, consider who you are embracing. When you are vigilant, you can progress better in life by what you are and are not accepting of. Many problems could have been prevented had people used wisdom and disconnected relationships when the signs were present.

Life has trials and tribulations, but you must know which trials are worth fighting for and the intent of the matter. Because of your decision to break the barriers of deception, you are leading the way for a generation who will look up to you to do the same. It takes a bold person, to stand up for what everyone else is afraid to. Be confident in this. He who began a good work in you will see it through to the end.

Take some time to meditate on the word of God, day and night, because, in your understanding of who you are, you will not fall for the bait of lies, manipulation, chaos, and flattery. God has gifted you with important tasks to do, and you must stay focused and not allow the disruption of the world to control your perception of life, identity, and purpose.

At times, your Faith may be tested, depending upon the challenge you face, but remember what God has done! Never forget it. Remind yourself that nothing can keep you hostage from God's promises when you are in God's will.

And do not be discouraged when you are fulfilling the plans of God. Remember the days, times, and seasons you live in. **Let no one deceive you. Read 2nd Timothy 3:1-9:**

" But know this, that in the last days perilous times will come: ² For men will be lovers of themselves, lovers of money, boasters, proud, blasphemers, disobedient to parents, unthankful, unholy, ³ unloving, unforgiving, slanderers,

without self-control, brutal, despisers of good, ⁴ traitors, headstrong, haughty, lovers of pleasure rather than lovers of God, ⁵ having a form of godliness but denying its power. And from such people turn away! ⁶ For of this sort are those who creep into households and make captives of gullible women loaded down with sins, led away by various lusts, ⁷ always

learning and never able to come to the knowledge of the truth. ⁸ Now as Jannes and Jambres resisted Moses, so do these also resist the truth: men of corrupt minds, disapproved concerning the faith; ⁹ but they will progress no further, for their folly will be manifest to all, as theirs also was." 2 Timothy 3: 1-9

DECEPTIVE PRACTICES

DECEPTIVE PRACTICES

I will summarize 8 Deceptive Practices that we must all be alert about so we can live a peaceful life not consumed by others' problems and inner plans.

REDIRECT

- People will redirect your path out of the will of God and try to disconnect you from the Spirit. They will also redirect your perception from life's reality to deception and delusion.

SEE OPPORTUNITY

- People will see you as the opportunity to get ahead. By any means, they create strategies behind what they want to happen.

RETWIST WORDS

- People will switch up the words you say to accommodate the narrative they want to spin. Mixing truths with lies to seem believable to deceive.

BETRAY

- Just like Judas betrayed Jesus, people will pay you close to weaponize what you share. They will feed you what you want to hear to chop you down with what you say.

START RUMORS

- People will spread false gossip and slander you to ruin your reputation and control how others view you to the point where you are unable to give a first impression.

  The plan is to weaken your credibility, where people will never believe what you have to say.

PLAY VICTIM

- People will be the first to throw rocks and share the story as if they were bruised, which strengthens their territory with the pity of others.

USE POWER

- People will use status and entitled nature to try and lessen your value to others to limit your resources.

THROW SPITE

- People will add smart remarks in conversation with others about you to plant seeds in the minds of others to act out impulsively.

PRAYER FOR WISDOM

Dear Heavenly Father,

I pray for everyone reading this prayer. I pray that you give them the wisdom to mature today. You said that you give wisdom to those who ask, and I pray that you increase them with it. I pray for their insight to know who is truly for them and who is not. As they walk with you, I pray that you remove anyone who is not meant for them. May you give them comfort as they transition to higher heights and greater. I pray that you give them the wisdom to know what to do in troublesome seasons. Allow them to accept the changes you placed in their life to fulfill the assignment. With much is given, much is required, and I pray that they have the wisdom to respond in a manner that is pleasing to you when they are tested. May their steps be ordered, and may they harken to your voice alone. I thank you for the plans you have for them.

I pray that they keep the Fear of The Lord in their hearts, minds, and hands so they can walk in wisdom despite living in a world that lacks it. I pray that they connect with like kind and destiny helpers sent by you to help them in their journey. I bind all attacks set against their mind and anything opposed to their future for them. May every attack be dis-positioned to dismay and shame. I thank you for all the things you have done.

Thank you in advance.

In Jesus Name

AMEN

REFLECTIONS

REFLECTIONS

Take a moment to reflect on your thoughts and takeaways that can apply in your life.

_____
_____
_____
_____
_____
_____
_____
_____
_____
_____
_____
_____
_____

WRITE YOUR OWN PRAYER

WRITE YOUR OWN PRAYER

AFFIRMATIONS

- I am loved by God and do not need the validation of others to feel accepted.

- I am important and will not allow others to use me as an opportunity, as I deserve to connect with those who genuinely care for me.

- I am becoming better each day. I have acknowledged that I am not perfect but God will perfect that which concerns me.

- I am confident in who I am and who God says I am. I destroy all word curses that oppose what God says about me.

- I am growing daily and will continue to build my relationship with God by reading His Word.

- I am deserving of truth and to connect with others who do not want to deceive me, to destruction, but to uplift me to higher.

- I am elevating, and prosperity is my portion as part of the inheritance of the Kingdom of God. I look forward to all the blessings with my name on it.

- I am called by God, and He knows me by name. He still chose me while in my struggles and favored me through it all. He takes everything personally regarding me.

- I am powerful, and I walk in God given authority, and I speak in confidence and boldness.

- I am protected by my Father, the Most High, and He will guard me from all wickedness, including deception and those who masquerade like light but in darkness.

- I am a child of God, and He has full authority in my life and controls what happens to me. I belong to the Lord.

- I am fearless because greater is He that is within me and protects me, the apple of His eye from all things.

- I am discerning, and God will gift me the knowledge to know who is for me and who is not.

- I am wise because the Lord instilled in me wisdom by the Fear of the Lord.

- I am appreciated by those who love me and those God called to me as destiny helpers. God always sends the help.

- I am strong and will not allow others to use my vulnerabilities as a weakness or a weapon to cause havoc in my life, for I can do all things through Christ who strengthens me.

7 DAY SELF PRAYERS AGAINST DECEPTION

7 DAY SELF PRAYERS AGAINST DECEPTION

Dear Heavenly Father,

DAY 1

I rest in you and free my mind from the worries of the world. I cast down all imaginations that go against your knowledge. I find peace with you, and I let go of the anxiousness that causes me to rush before your time. You said at the right time you will make it happen, so I renew my strength in you. When I am empty, you make me whole. I bind all word curses, and I speak against it with the word of God. I break the barriers of all lies said against me. May all lies be put to shame. Lies meant to destroy my purpose, future, and self-security. I block all attacks against word curses, known and unknown; I smite the enemy with blindness. God, I pray that your consuming fire surrounds me from all lies intended to weaken me; by your Spirit, my strength is perfected.

In Jesus Name,

AMEN

7 DAY SELF PRAYERS AGAINST DECEPTION

Dear Heavenly Father,

DAY 2

I thank you for shielding me from the attacks of the enemy.

The enemy has been busy, but you are greater and all-powerful. God, I ask that you protect me from all deception that may be in my circle. I pray you to reveal the hands of all those close to me and protect me from hidden traps set for my defeat. God, I pray that you reveal to me the things I do not know. Despite how painful it may be for me, I pray you give me the comfort to accept all truth. God, I pray that you will contend against all monitoring spirits looking to pry information to use against me. You said your eyes are on the righteous, and I thank you for always watching over me. May your right hand uphold me, and may I embrace your presence daily as I hide in you.

In Jesus Name,

AMEN

7 DAY SELF PRAYERS AGAINST DECEPTION

Dear Heavenly Father,

DAY 3

I thank you for the thoughts that you have towards me, even in my imperfections. In you, I am made whole. I am beautifully and wonderfully made by you. I am the apple of your eye, and I thank you for covering me. I pray that I remain aligned with your will. I pray I keep my ears to Heaven and focus on you and no one else. I pray that the desire to grow in you strengthens daily. I pray against all attacks of deception and weaken the camp of the enemy every day. You are my anchor, and I put my full trust in you. I pray against anyone who looks to take advantage of me and sees me as an advancement with no care for me at all. I pray for discernment to know who is for me and who is not. Teach me to discern people, places, and things. May nothing go beyond my prophetic awareness, and I accept all the red flags as warning signs.

In Jesus Name,

AMEN

7 DAY SELF PRAYERS AGAINST DECEPTION

Dear Heavenly Father,

DAY 4

I thank you for this new day filled with new mercies. I thank you for protecting me and my family against seen and unseen. I thank you for the supernatural strength that gets me through each day. I know I am nothing without you and I thank you for uplifting me during times I feel I cannot see my way. I pray against the works of deception and I ask that the seeded sprouts of people are made visible to me. I pray that you expose all hidden things plotting destruction. May the fire of God respond against all things hidden. I am more than a conqueror because of your love. I bind all manipulation and confusion, trying to cause chaos. I destroy the yoke of evil and the workers of iniquity. Deception is destroyed and will not reign in my life any longer. I put on the full armor of God against the evil works, and it shall not prevail against me because you are for me. I thank you, God, for all of these things and the ways you have made for me.

In Jesus Name,

AMEN

Dear Heavenly Father,

DAY 5

I thank you for freedom and for breaking the chains that tried to hold me down. I thank you, God for the renewing of my mind, so I can think and see clearly. I bind the holds of self-deception and anything I believed to be true and was not. I ask for forgiveness if I ever believed in a lie and did not like the truth. I pray against moving ahead of your time because of excitement; I will wait for you. May my mind and heart stay pleasing in your sight, protect me from my own self-deception, and bring truth in revelation. Thank you in advance.

In Jesus Name,

Amen

7 DAY SELF PRAYERS AGAINST DECEPTION

Dear Heavenly Father,

DAY 6

You have not given me the spirit of fear but of power. I thank you for joy and peace. I destroy all attacks of deception that come through fear, intimidation, and provoking spirits. I destroy the yoke by the blood of Jesus. No weapon formed against me shall prosper. I thank you for the things that you blocked from reaching me and stopped it in its tracks. I thank you for protecting my family from spiritual attacks meant to cause division and poverty. I stand in the gap for my family and loved ones, and I pray your angels take charge of them. I cancel the assignments of worry by the blood of Jesus. I stand in authority, dominion, and power.

In Jesus Name,

AMEN

7 DAY SELF PRAYERS AGAINST DECEPTION

Dear Heavenly Father,

DAY 7

I thank you that our Faith heals, and by our Faith you are pleased. I have the Faith to believe that all things work for me who loves you and is called according to your purpose. I have the Faith to believe that you will lift up a standard when the enemy comes in like a flood. I have the Faith to believe your plans are to prosper me. I have the Faith to believe you will contend with those that contend against me. I have the Faith to believe I can do all things through Christ, who strengthens me. I have the Faith to believe you will protect me from the hands of evildoers and their deception. I have the Faith God Almighty. I thank you for all the things that have been done in your Name. You are my provider, healer, protector, and strength, and you make all things work. I will forever give you the Glory and the Honor and the Praise forever. May you bless my future, and may I delight in your presence for the rest of my days.

In Jesus Name,

AMEN

BACK TEXT

There are different doors of deception, and this book will help identify areas where deception may present as "good opportunities". We prepare the caring and bold hearts to navigate life without being easily deceived.

In a world filled with corruption, it is challenging to navigate through the chaos without clear insight from God. Many live in regret, and this guide will help prevent years of bad decisions and a life of error.

We share essential keys to discern people, places, and things and help to identify what is most important.

Your life is valuable to God, and He has a plan for you, that requires you to walk in your God-Given Identity by clothing yourself in His righteousness.

I pray that God will open your spiritual eyes to see the world surrounding you and idle words will not deceive you.

"I will give you the treasures of darkness And hidden riches of secret places, That you may know that I, the LORD, Who call *you* by your name, *Am* the God of Israel." Isaiah 45: 3

ABOUT THE AUTHOR

Jamille Judge is a certified Relationship Coach, Our Faith Heals LLC, and Our Faith Connects founder. She believes fully in the power of the Living God and that we have complete salvation through His son, Jesus Christ. Jamille encourages others to activate their divine calling and purpose on Earth. She emphasizes the importance of connection with the Trinity (God, The Son, and the Holy Spirit), which provides clarity, wisdom, direction, protection, peace, power, authority, and purpose in a World filled with darkness, wickedness, and destruction. She believes God has called us to be a light to shine as an example of love in a cruel world by using wisdom in life. She shows love in her community by connecting and emphasizing the importance of creating healthy relationships by sharing the Word of God and building up the community through the needs and resources.

www.ourfaithheals.com

www.ourfaithconnects.com

www.ingramcontent.com/pod-product-compliance
Lightning Source LLC
Chambersburg PA
CBHW052032030426
42337CB00027B/4962